Applying the Branding Iron

Applying the Branding Iron

Kartikeya Kompella

Viva Books
New Delhi | Mumbai | Chennai | Kolkata | Bangalore | Hyderabad | Kochi | Guwahati

First Published 2006
Reprinted 2009

VIVA BOOKS PRIVATE LIMITED

- 4737/23 Ansari Road, Daryaganj, New Delhi 110 002
  E-mail: vivadelhi@vivagroupindia.net, Tel. 42242200
- 76, Service Industries, Shirvane, Sector 1, Nerul, Navi Mumbai 400 706
  E-mail: vivamumbai@vivagroupindia.net, Tel. 27721273, 27721274
- Jamals Fazal Chambers, 26 Greams Road, Chennai 600 006
  E-mail: vivachennai@vivagroupindia.net, Tel. 28290304, 28294241
- B-103, Jindal Towers, 21/1A/3 Darga Road, Kolkata 700 017
  E-mail: vivakolkata@vivagroupindia.net, Tel. 22836381, 22816713
- 7, Sovereign Park Apartments, 56-58, K. R. Road, Basavanagudi, Bangalore 560 004
  E-mail: vivabangalore@vivagroupindia.net, Tel. 26607409, 26607410
- 101-102 Mughal Marc Apartments, 3-4-637 to 641, Narayanguda, Hyderabad 500 029
  E-mail: vivahyderabad@vivagroupindia.net, Tel. 27564481, 27564482
- First Floor, Beevi Towers, SRM Road, Kaloor, Kochi 682 018, Kerala
  E-mail: vivakochi@vivagroupindia.net, Tel: 0484-2403055, 2403056
- H. No. 12, P. B. Road, Near Arya Hospital, Rehabari, Guwahati 781 008
  E-mail: vivaguwahati@vivagroupindia.net, Tel: 0361-2735624

www.vivagroupindia.com

ISBN: 978-81-309-0194-7

Published by Vinod Vasishtha for Viva Books Private Limited, 4737/23, Ansari Road, Daryaganj, New Delhi - 110 002.

Printed and bound by Raj Press, R-3 Inderpuri, New Delhi - 110 012.

CONTENTS

To Mom and Dad

Preface

In 2001, 10 years after I started my career, I was surprised and delighted to receive an invitation to present a paper at the ESOMAR/ARF Conference on Online Measurement in Athens. I was even more delighted when at the end of the conference my paper was nominated for the John & Mary Goodyear Award for Excellence in International Market Research. This gave me the confidence to start writing articles on my favourite subject – branding. When my first article became the recommended reading for a few MBA courses in the US and Canada, I was encouraged to start sending some of my papers to branding experts. They were extremely kind in taking time off to read the papers of a complete stranger and saw merit in my work.

In the meantime I had become a part of various international discussion forums on branding and was writing for various branding websites. A small but growing set of well-wishers were asking me to compile my papers into a book, which is the product you see in front of you.

Applying the Branding Iron is a collection of papers and articles that I have written on topics that interest me about branding. They are not sequential or necessarily linked to each other in any manner. I have tried to keep them simple, clear and interesting. I hope that they will be useful to the reader and show how varied, rich and alive this subject is.

I would like to thank the editors of the different sites that have published my writings for giving me the opportunity to write for them and for their constant encouragement. Many thanks to Robin Rusch, Elen Lewis, Ren Spiteri, Danielle Blumenthal and Christine Arden. I would also like to thank Professor Philip Kotler, Professor Jagdish Sheth, Simon Anholt, Scott Davis, Chris Macrae, Jack Yan, SiccoVan Gelder, Ray George, Lynn Upshaw, Tim Ambler, Nancy Lee and Tom Blackett for their comments and suggestions on papers I sent them. Special thanks to *www.brandchannel.com* for allowing me to reproduce in this book my article 'What's Wrong with Brands These Days?' that originally appeared on the Brandchannel site. All opinions expressed in this book are my personal and do not reflect the views of my organisation.

I hope you enjoy this book and find it useful. Do mail me your feedback and suggestions at:

kartik@buildingbrandmeaning.com

1

Applying the Branding Iron

BRANDING is one of the most powerful concepts of the twentieth century. People look at brands from the perspective of employees, as producers of goods and services, as investment options, as causes to be supported, etc. The concept of branding has been around for centuries, but the explosion of markets, media, marketing and communication in the twentieth century has taken branding to a completely stratospheric level.

Branding has come a long way from the days when hot irons were applied to reluctant cattle in the attempt to depict ownership by creating a differentiating mark on the unfortunate cattle. Modern day branding is still about creating a differentiating mark, but now the mark is to be made in the minds of the consumers and other audiences, using a less-violent method. Applying the branding iron is not as easy as it was, though some simple and memorable lessons remain relevant to this day.

In the modern context, branding is the process of creating and maintaining a relationship between an 'offering' and its audience that can be leveraged to a commercial end. 'Offerings' could be anything from products or services to the promises of a better future made by a political party.

Strong brands are driven by the genuine intent of the brand custodian to provide an offering of value to the audience, and this 'offering' is noticed because it is seen as different from competition and is believed to be relevant to the audiences' requirement. The offering presents a set of values that are relevant to the audiences' context and therefore strikes a chord. The consistency of these values enhances the life of the brand as these values form the basis of the brand promise and identity.

For example, Disney is a brand that is over eighty years old. It was started by a person who had a genuine intent to provide entertainment. The operating values here were that Disney would provide wholesome, high quality family entertainment. This brand promise has been recognised as different yet extremely relevant, and this consistency of values has made Disney a much-respected brand over the years the world over.

Despite branding seeming to be an extremely complex subject, many have built brands with little or no formal knowledge of the subject. Some of the biggest brands are over a 100 years old. Their early custodians probably had no formal literature on the subject – only sound values and genuine intent. Much of branding is commonsensical as has been demonstrated by brands like Disney, Wal-Mart and Dell. These all are brands that were started by ambitious entrepreneurs with no formal 'brand' training.

The brand custodians of these brands were focused on delivering great value to their customers and directed their organisations' energies towards achieving their brand promise, and in doing so created not only a great brand in terms of marketing but also great organisations built on sound values. And indeed great brands are not just about slick marketing but creating relationships that endure. Brands have many audiences including existing and prospective employees, investors, the public at large, the government, to mention a few. A flaw in any aspect of the brand, whether it is sexual harassment of workers or non-compliance with environmental standards, can hurt a brand's relationship with its audience (read brand equity). Relationships are built over time and through diligently sticking to the brand promise.

Brands can only deliver according to their brand promise if the organisational processes are working in its favour. It is probably fitting that organisations take an organisational perspective to branding as the benefits of branding impact many aspects of an organisation. A good brand leverages its equity in a variety of ways from using the brand name to get high-quality employees on board to getting soft financing from the market. There are many tools brands use to grow stronger – some are well known but not always used well, like websites, while others are not so well known, like the use of heritage, tradition and advocacy in building brands. There are also many things that brands do wrong that hurt their equity and these serve as lessons for others.

A lot of progress in brand theory has come about by analysing the key factors that drive brand successes and failures. Through analysis of existing brands, one can identify concepts like heritage brands; one can understand how brands have used stories to build interest, relevance and differentiation; one can understand the principles that drive advocacy and the principles behind cause-related branding. These concepts are explained in the chapters to follow. As is seen across brands, the principles remain the same, but their priority and the key issues may vary from category to category.

Similarly, it is important to understand some of the key issues in different forms of branding in order to appreciate the complexity of branding in different categories. Identifying the key issues is important before implementing a branding exercise as it places the entire task in perspective. The success of many politicians, celebrities, etc. was that they understood these issues instinctively. These issues may vary across categories – in celebrity branding the key issue may be of how to maintain relevance with an audience that is changing, whereas in the branding of colas the key issue may be that of how to maintain differentiation and attract customers generation after generation without losing focus, consistency or appeal.

The task of branding in different categories is very interesting. Branding of celebrities is of interest to many because it is the branding of human beings. Branding of non-profits is important because these non-profits play an important role in helping people and most non-profits need all the support they can get. The branding of political parties is fascinating because many politicians are instinctively good at touching a chord with their audience and can position themselves and reposition competition brilliantly and can actually teach marketers a thing or two. Pharma branding can vary in its complexity based on whether the brand is prescription based or not.

The scope of branding has grown immensely over the years to move from purely a marketing function to an organisational function. Its richness and importance can only grow stronger as it involves more and more aspects of life and management.

2

Can Story-Telling Help Your Brand?

'A TALE well told always finds eager listeners,' goes the storyteller's saying. Whether it is the dusty marketplace of the Arabian lands or the dingy surroundings of a waterfront pub – a good tale is always appreciated.

Story-telling is an ancient art and a powerful tool. Stories have the power to inspire knaves to be heroes and to turn beggars to kings. Whether a tragedy or a comedy – a good story can always stir human emotions. Allegories, parables and fables have been used to teach specific lessons. A good story has the power to draw attention, build interest, deeply involve the listener, teach and have strong recall.

With so many benefits to a good tale, there is good reason for brand managers to use story-telling techniques for branding. Stories can be used to build familiarity or esteem; they can be used to reinforce relevance or drive home brand differentiation. After all, interesting stories about brands will find ready listeners. These stories can build brand relationships that are strong and enduring.

This technique is not new. However, it finds itself greater relevance in the case of wannabes and glamour related semi-brands. Newspapers, magazines and tabloids are replete with true and sometimes not-very-true stories on film stars, rock stars and the like that add to these stars' appeal. Similarly, interesting little-known facts about famous personalities add to the interest value of the personality concerned.

There are a variety of areas about which brands can give interesting information. Some of these are given below:

1. Who uses it ?

Celebrities who use the brand could make for interesting stories. It is interesting to know that hard-muscled film actor Arnold Schwarzenegger sports a Timex and so does the beautiful actress with the Mensa mind, Sharon Stone. This brings to mind some interesting questions like: Which brand of cigars did Churchill smoke or What brand of coffee is served on the sets of the hit serial *Friends*? These kinds of stories give consumers the feeling, 'if it was good enough for them it is good enough for me' and creates strong quality connotations while providing strong image differentiation. This also makes consumers feel warmer about the brand.

2. Where is it used?

It is said that Jockey undergarments were recommended by NASA for astronauts to ensure that they did not face any discomfort while travelling in space. This information would have great interest value for people living in countries where Jockey is still relatively unknown. This would act as a strong testimony of the brand's quality. The fact that the brand is over 125 years old also adds to the interest value of the brand, not to forget that this also speaks volumes for the brand's durability (no pun intended) and heritage.

Brands need to hunt out stories and use them for their benefit. For example, there's bound to be a detergent that is used in the Buckingham Palace and used for a good reason. The brand that is used could go to town talking of how it is the detergent used for the royalty's clothes. This trick again works in creating quality connotations and emphasising differentiation.

3. What was it used for?

There is a popular, often misquoted, story of how a consumer used the light from his Timex Indiglo to guide a group of people down over several flights of stairs during a blackout. The exact details may have been lost to memory, but the story remains as an exciting testimonial of the brand's utility.

4. How was it promoted?

It is not popular knowledge amongst consumers that Coke was once promoted as an ideal brain tonic. The knowledge that Coca Cola was apparently once promoted as a tonic makes for interesting information and adds to the strong sense of heritage and reinforces the association of Coca Cola with the evolution of America. Nostalgia and novelty is a rarity for many brands and if you have it, flaunt it! Such examples show pedigree, longevity and a continuous relevance amongst audiences over the years – in this case it also probably helps establish a clear distance between the brand and its 'teeny-bopper' competitors.

5. Who invented it?

Everyone knows that Thomas Edison invented the light bulb, but not many know that he founded the multi-billion-dollar corporation GE. While this knowledge may not make people flock to the stores to buy GE offerings, it does make for interesting information, displays heritage and helps memorability. Many people do not know of the relationship between Graham Bell and Bell Corporation.

6. Tales of heroism and valour

A watch that defied the ravages of sea water for 10 years, a battery that miraculously kept a clock going for 12 years, a bulb that did not burn out for 15 years. These are records worthy of the proudest record book – these are tales that some brands can tell. These are tales that make consumers look at the brand with a newfound respect. These tales aid recall value and are good for word-of-mouth publicity. Importantly, these stories add character to the brand and powerfully reinforce the brand's claim of quality.

7. Rituals & traditions

Stories like how Wal-Mart's CEO danced the hula on Wall Street when Wal-Mart's pretax profits reached eight percent of sales and how a Wal-Mart manager wrestled a bear when he lost a bet show the human side of the brand. Consumers like brands that have a human side and relate to warm workplace stories.

What these interesting pieces of information also do is help create brand familiarity and involvement with consumers. It adds a little something by way of differentiation and adds to the recall value while strongly emphasising commitment in an interesting and credible manner. Importantly, they add emotion and warmth to the brand – often an underrated quality in an increasingly commercial world.

It is important for brands to look at what tales they have to tell the consumers. Looking at their own history is a good way to start. Keeping a ready ear for interesting tales is also very important. Coke and Timex have a repertoire of real-life customer anecdotes about their brands that are enjoyable and heartwarming. These brands are aware that they have become a part of popular culture and ask consumers to send in interesting real-life stories involving these brands to strengthen their role as a part of popular culture.

It is important for brands to use opportunities that help create a piece of their own history. Being the pen used to sign an important document like the US President's acceptance of office can create history for a brand. (It possibly would be a good thing not to commercialise the occasion by being the 'official pen', but use this information as a piece of brand history.) Similarly, being the shirt brand worn by a businessman while making a revolutionary announcement can help create brand history.

If your brand has stories to tell, tell them true, tell them loud and tell them well. Consumers will listen keenly and reward your brand for the lore that surrounds it.

3

Why Should Brands Build Traditions?

TRADITION is an important component of culture. While the benefits of tradition are not immediately evident, tradition offers brand custodians a powerful tool for brand building. Tradition plays an important role in the lives of people, which is why tradition continues to thrive in many countries.

The importance of tradition lies in the fact that it helps provide and reinforce identity. It helps mark special occasions and binds together total strangers participating in common traditions. Traditions create a sense of stability and provide a feeling of reassurance to their participants. The pleasure that many derive from family get-togethers on Christmas Eve and Thanksgiving dinners and the powerful emotions experienced at Independence Day celebrations are strong indicators that tradition can have a strong and enduring impact on people. As long as it is meaningful, enjoyable and heart warming, most people tend to appreciate tradition. Tradition offers marketers cues for creating enduring brand properties.

A brand tradition is a tradition created by a brand that adds a strong experiential element to the brand and that adds to the overall equity of the brand. McDonald's tradition of service within a specified time or money back has become integral to the brand. In a way brand traditions create a set of 'good memories' for customers to look back on.

A brand may have a set of existing practices that make for strong traditions, or it can consider consciously creating practices that can become traditions for the brand. In order to elevate a practice to a tradition it is important for the practice to be implemented consistently over a period of time. Brands can even take over popular traditions by sponsoring them. In the Netherlands it has been a tradition since the mid 1960s for people to take a dip in the North Sea at the seaside town of Scheveningen on New Year's day. Unox Soup has apparently in recent years linked into this event by sponsoring the event and dishing out hot soup and branded woolly hats to participants. There apparently is even a website dedicated to it with pictures.

Traditions have connotations that are useful to brands as well and give strong reasons for brands to create their own traditions:

1. Consistency

Traditions are a symbol of consistency in an ever-changing world. Consistency is the essence of branding – brands are preferred over their generic counterparts because of the consistency of value and quality that is expected from brands. Creating or maintaining traditions reinforces the constituents' perception of the brand's consistency.

2. Commitment to values

The values that a brand represents form the basis of the brand's relationship with its consumers. Consumers expect brands to be committed to these values, and to the relationship as well. Creating and sustaining brand traditions shows a brand's commitment to its values. The solidity of resolve in sticking to tradition demonstrates the brand's powerful and reassuring impact on consumers.

3. Providing a good brand experience

If a brand tradition is successful, it provides a memorable brand experience and adds to the overall brand experience. A vintage car rally by a car manufacturer or an annual exhibition of futuristic writing instruments by a large writing instruments company can possibly serve as brand traditions if they suit the brand and the prevailing culture of the land. These kinds of brand traditions would possibly be enjoyed and looked forward to by consumers.

4. Reaffirmation of identity

Brand traditions by their very practice and repetition state and reaffirm a brand's identity. The 'Swoosh' identifies Nike and the controversial issues that Bennetton addresses in its ads identify Bennetton. Similarly, a brand tradition becomes a unique part of the brand's identity.

The tennis tournament Wimbledon is a good example of how tradition has become an integral part of a brand's identity. Arguably the most respected tennis tournament in the world, Wimbledon is a strong brand in its own right. Its brand equity is largely drawn from the fact that the tournament is steeped in tradition. Players tend to be better behaved and more inhibited in their expression of displeasure towards the occasional unfavourable ruling by umpires at tennis' premier championship. At Wimbledon, unlike many other tournaments where the heights and depths of sports fashion are visible, the apparel worn by players is always white and according to the rigid dress code decreed by the tournament officials.

The customary bowing of players to the royal box, the presence of the Duchess of Kent and the serving of strawberries and cream are traditions that add to the charm of Wimbledon. It is the tradition that makes Wimbledon so special to players and spectators alike and despite the fickle weather and the many restrictions, being at Wimbledon is perceived to be an experience to treasure.

Brand traditions could be simple yet very effective. Here are some examples:

1. Nilgiris

A popular confectionery chain in Bangalore conducts an annual cake exhibition that is the talk of the town. Cakes designed in innovative shapes and sizes that extend up to 80 feet in length are displayed at this festival. Some of these cakes reflect contemporary topics with cakes designed as battletanks or cakes featuring interesting graphics made out of icing sugar such as scenes from a cricket match. The exhibition is very popular and is usually packed with families eager to see the exhibits.

2. Ben & Jerry's offers free ice cream on Free Cone Day

This is a tradition that the brand started and despite the number of free cones running into over three hundred thousand in a year, the brand continues to stick to this tradition that has become an integral part of the brand's identity.

Creating brand traditions requires an understanding of what makes some traditions relevant and enduring and others short-lived. Here are some of the important aspects of traditions that brands must keep in mind.

1. Tradition has to become a part of popular culture

To be successful any tradition has to become a part of popular culture. The test of the tradition is its ability to become a symbol of popular culture. The success of Nilgiris cake festival can be attributed to the festival quickly becoming a part of the city's culture.

2. Tradition should retain its significance

There are several traditions that have lost their significance over the years. Traditions that started centuries ago due to circumstances prevailing then may no longer be relevant today. If a brand tradition loses its significance, then it will die out very soon. It is important to ensure that the significance is maintained by creating subtle changes that preserve the tradition's continuing relevance. For example, if a vintage car rally starts losing its significance, then the brand may add significance to this tradition by using physically challenged seniors as car drivers and position the rally as a celebration of the triumph of the human spirit.

3. Tradition should have involvement

Tradition has to be noticed and appreciated. For this a sense of involvement is required. A marathon run generates a lot of involvement. Similarly eating strawberries and cream at Wimbledon is an act of tradition but involves the visitor.

4. Traditions need to be contemporary

Traditions need not be boring and archaic. A contemporary society is accustomed to contemporary expression and brands need to reflect modernity while retaining the essence of a tradition.

5. Traditions need to make one feel warm about them

Traditions that touch one's heart are more resilient than others.

Christmas eve get-togethers and New Year parties are testimony to this. Brands need to ensure that their traditions spark off warm feelings amongst their constituents.

Brands need to audit their existing practices to see if there are any practices that can be continued as traditions. A good way of evaluating whether a practice can become a tradition is to examine whether it adds to the brand's equity and helps create a unique and distinct identity. Alternatively, brands can look at creating tradition based on their understanding of what would embody the brand's values and personality while merging into popular culture. Brands need to look at whatever they do from the perspective of whether it is 'traditionable' in the long run. For example, if a charity-based sale is going to be conducted, the brand should look at whether this sale has the potential to become a strong tradition if run year after year.

An intended brand tradition only becomes a tradition once it is practised for some time, and this is good as it enables testing before the decision to 'traditionise' is taken. The relative success/failure of this practice in achieving the desired objectives can be measured over time. If it appears that this practice will endure the test of time, then brand custodians can give it all the support that a brand property deserves. The decision to create a tradition, however, must be taken carefully because withdrawing a brand tradition after it has been maintained for some time can have negative repercussions for the brand.

Brand traditions enhance the brand, satisfy the consumers and sometimes redefine popular culture. A brand that can create traditions that become a part of popular culture arguably has the potential to last as long as the culture does.

4

20 Steps to Creating Powerful Brand Websites

MOST brand custodians recognise the power of the web as a tool for branding. The versatility that technology provides, the ease of operation that the web offers, the immense amount of relevant information that can be communicated simply yet impactfully give brand custodians good reasons to set up websites for their brands. (These websites are called 'brand' websites or 'branding' websites.) Often, to maximise the impact from the website brand custodians try too hard, and the result is often a brand website that delivers an under-par brand experience.

There are several articles on the use of websites as tools for branding – some dwell on technology and others on the philosophy of 'branding' websites – but few articles explain the required perspective to developing brand-based websites and the simple guidelines involved in developing effective 'brand' websites. While the volume of information at hand can sometimes be intimidating, at other times articles exaggerate the complexity of the task. The perceived need for understanding technology and the use of terms like 'intuitive navigation' makes the task of creating a good website seem terribly complex and requiring enormous effort.

Several articles written on the use of websites in brand building are idealistic and set the minimum acceptable level of brand websites too high for brand custodians to wish to set up a website for their brands. It is not surprising that many brand custodians either do not put up a website for their brand or alternatively put up a shoddy site that is termed as an 'interim' site.

This chapter is an attempt to specify areas that will help brand custodians develop websites that work for their brands. The emphasis is on optimising, not maximising, the potential of the web for a brand through its website; maximising is the next step based on each custodian's resources level.

The following 20 steps can help create powerful brand websites:

1. Express the brand's personality

The ease with which brands can communicate their personality through their website is amazing (though most people opt for the tougher and more complex approach). Identity and personality can be conjured up through simple effects. Something as simple as the voice of the celebrity endorsing the brand welcoming the site visitor to the site could itself have a powerful impact on the site visitor. Offline design elements and brand properties carried online can provide a familiar and welcoming feel to the site. *www.nike.com* is a good example of how a brand can communicate brand image and personality powerfully through their website. Consumers often appreciate the fact that the brand has maintained consistency and has not been seduced by the web into creating a radically different e-personality.

2. Content first, tech next

It is not always essential to have a hi-techno scream-blast effect on site visitors. Research indicates that there are many surfers who are not very technology friendly and that there are many novice surfers joining the ranks of the Internet every day. Too many hi-tech effects requiring downloads of software from different sites can intimidate these surfers.

A surfer who is not very Internet savvy would most likely be seeking reassurance from brands as familiar faces in an unfamiliar environment. A complicated hi-tech site may leave the visitor bewildered and not too happy about the online brand experience. Sometimes less can do more with many surfers finding hi-tech effects a poor substitute for meaningful content. Giving the visitor options to view the site in basic or hi-effect form would be a much-appreciated feature. Hi-tech effects can be demonstrated in the hi-tech effect version.

3. Emphasise differentiation

Research indicates that most brands derive their equity from their differentiation from competition. The brand's website needs to drive this differentiation home, which is the basis of the consumer–brand relationship. Differentiation is integral to the brand's DNA – everything that represents the brand has to reflect the differentiation. Whether it is price differentiation or even image differentiation – differentiation can easily be emphasised powerfully through brand websites. Some websites give elaborate explanations of how their brand offers significant economies to their consumers while other brands use websites to explain the brand's tradition of quality to create image-based differentiation.

4. Ensure that the site reflects the brand's values

Every brand has a unique set of values that forms its very essence. Communicating these values through the website is of paramount importance as this is the charter of the brand. Knowing the brand's values and the direction of its charter is important to anyone who wishes to have an enduring relationship with the brand. The website gives interested visitors an opportunity to understand these values better and the opportunity to forge a more meaningful relationship with the brand's constituents.

5. Information about the brand

Many surfers visit brand sites to know about the brand – its antecedents, its vision, etc. Irrespective of whether site visitors want to know about the brand or not, it is always reassuring to have an 'About Us' section as this indicates transparency and openness.

Details of offices, locations, email ids, nature of ownership of the company, place and date of incorporation, number of years in existence, etc. are always available through offline sources to people who really want them. Putting up these facts in an easily navigable manner gives visitors a feeling of confidence and transparency that is very important especially in today's environment of low trust levels. Analysts, media people, potential employees/ investors /associates and channel partners find this section of immense use – and these are important audiences for a brand.

6. Education on brand selection

A large number of people visiting brand websites do so in order to understand whether the brand is relevant to them or not. Education on brand choice should not be restricted to stating your brand's case. At times consumers may not know whether they need the category itself.

Consumers need to be educated on the different categories of products that can serve their needs in the context in which they are planning to use your brand. A consumer who is looking at a brand of paint may not know that he actually needs distemper for that particular application and not paint itself. A brand may lose out on a sale by providing such information, but it can earn appreciation and positive WOM through this route that in time can bring in more sales.

7. Product specifications

Many prospective consumers want to know the product specifications of brands. Knowing the tolerance levels for industrial products, side effects for healthcare formulations, presence of a specific ingredient for edible products, etc. is critical for decision making. Equally important for a brand is communicating the kind of tests conducted for product quality and the brand's performance on these parameters. For example, if a cement brand is supposed to withstand 53 kilos of weight per square inch to qualify for a certain grade, then consumers may want to know whether the brand qualifies for this grade convincingly or only scrapes through in the performance test.

Many strong brands soar above the required quality levels while competition barely exceeds the quality levels. Some brands have ethical quality levels that are far higher than the government/industry specified levels. Websites give brands a good opportunity to share this kind of information that helps prospects/consumers develop a better appreciation of the brand.

8. Best uses

It is commonly believed that no one knows how to get the

best out of a brand more than the company manufacturing the brand. Giving tips on the best way to use the brand is a good way of convincing consumers about the brand's commitment to its consumers. Maintenance tips too help in terms of reassuring consumers of the brand's intent to play fair with the consumer.

9. Suggest more uses for the brand

Informing consumers of more uses for the brand helps to increase brand usage and consequently drives higher sales. But importantly, this information is of great use to consumers who are comfortable with the usage of a brand. These consumers may therefore prefer using the same brand for other purposes rather than using a different brand for these purposes. Web pages with such forms of relevant information add tremendously to providing a positive brand experience online.

10. Education related to the need satisfied

In some areas many marketers are short sighted. They are so pre-occupied in their marketing function that they do not recognise the fact that consumers buy their brand to satisfy a need. In this context, information pertaining to that need is welcome. If the brand offers skin-care solutions, consumers of the brand would welcome information on skin care and different means of taking care of one's skin. Providing such information also demonstrates the brand's expertise and commitment to consumers needs.

11. Brand heritage

There are many brands that have an interesting heritage but do not speak of it on the site, not knowing that it makes for interesting reading as well as enhances the brand's credibility. Brand heritage also builds greater familiarity with the brand. If a brand can talk of its past – who started it, how it started and how it evolved over the years – then consumers get a sense of the brand's history and a more appreciative perspective of the brand. Many consumers in Asia do not know that Thomas Alva Edison was one of the founders of GE or that Carrier is the company that invented air conditioners – information that adds to these brands' stature.

12. Give out interesting news about the brand

Brand extensions, forthcoming events, celebrities coming on board need to be up on the site. While it may seem obvious that this information should be carried on the website, it is disappointing to see that many big brands do not remember to include this information online until it is stale.

13. Who else uses the brand

Consumers derive great satisfaction in using brands that celebrities use. Often this sense of satisfaction is enhanced if the celebrity is not paid to endorse the brand. Knowing that Sharon Stone uses a Timex can add to the brand appeal or just to the consumer's pride of ownership.

14. Give interesting anecdotes about the brand

Many brands have witnessed interesting incidents that have gone on to become the brand's folklore. Timex has a set of real-life tales of the almost-death-defying resilience of the watch. Stories of how the watch has endured tough circumstances and come out ticking inspire awe for the brand. Brand custodians should use the brand website to communicate interesting brand tales to their prospects/consumers.

15. Put photographs of people

The presence of photographs speaks a lot for the credibility and friendliness of a brand. Photographs of the company headquarters and some key people add to the interest value of the site. The picture of the tea taster of a tea brand or the programmer behind a complex software brand makes for interesting viewing and costs next to nothing to put up.

16. Database creation

A common fault many big brands commit is asking site visitors for email ids without having a definite plan of how to use these in the near future. Often brands do not want to miss out on collecting email ids of visitors to their site, but do not realise that site visitors who give their email id normally do so expecting something in return, at least a simple newsletter. Not receiving anything in return for giving the brand permission to intrude into their life can cause rancour. Asking for email ids only makes sense if the brand has a ready plan of what to do with these ids in the future.

17. Ask for suggestions and reward them

Asking for suggestions is a sign of showing that the brand is not bigger than its well-wishers. A 'suggestions' section provides an interactive component to the website and can be of great value with the insights and advice that it elicits. Good suggestions can be rewarded with a simple gift and all suggestions should be rewarded with a mail thanking the contributor for the suggestion.

18. Ask for feedback and set deadlines for response

The feedback section of most sites is often the section that causes the most frustration with feedback either not responded to in a timely manner or just ignored. Unanswered complaints/queries can cause enormous irritation. This can be prevented through a simple line that states the time by which the brand's representative will reply. Creating a system of accountability for response to mails within the stipulated deadlines should not be too difficult for any brand.

19. Careers etiquette

Brands that have a careers section need to be discreet in the way they handle this section. People responding to the careers section can feel slighted if they do not receive any response for a while or ever. Auto response through bots is not a great way of providing response either. Applicants can be touchy, and getting a dehumanised auto response can rub them the wrong way. It is important to be sure before setting up this section whether the HR department has the interest and energy to handle online applications or not.

20. Allow business associates to contact you

A good website offers something for all its audiences. Giving prospective business associates an opportunity to communicate with the brand makes for common-sense marketing. Similarly, a section that provides information contact details for investors/media people is a part of every well-thought-out website.

The extent of information that the site can provide knows no boundaries. Many visitors of brand websites are seekers of information. The brand must ensure that they are not disappointed. As much relevant non-confidential information as can be provided should be available to interested site visitors. If the visitor is willing to search for it, then the brand should be willing to provide it. If the information required is too micro-detailed, then of course the visitor should be asked to send an email asking for the information.

Setting up a good website is only half the task. Poor maintenance, non-working links, grammatical mistakes, irregular updating and non-responses to consumer mails are but some of the many mistakes that several big brands make. Proper delineation of responsibility amongst the team responsible for the site, attention to detail and commitment to meeting deadlines to issues such as site updation, response to mails, etc. are what make a brand's website work for the brand.

The decision to set up a website for a brand is a strategic decision and requires commitment and attention to make the effort successful. Like any other strategic initiative, the website requires adequate management time and resources to yield the requisite benefits. A website backed by insufficient resources could be counterproductive to the brand. As the saying goes, 'The bigger the weapon the more dangerous it is when it misfires.'

5

How to Use 'Causes' to Build Brand Equity

THERE are many benefits to being perceived as socially responsible, and so brands are putting in many efforts to be seen as socially responsible or just as 'good guys'. The quickest and probably easiest way of doing this is by being associated with a good cause. This association shows the brand to be responsible and caring, and these are indeed good qualities for a brand to have.

While some brands are inspired by a genuine sense of social responsibility, many brands look at the image of being socially responsible as helping in building brand stature. The conscious employment of resources by a brand to aid charitable causes in order to develop image, associations and identity benefits is called cause-related branding.

In addition to the moral satisfaction of doing the right thing, there are business reasons that also drive brands' association with causes. Not all brands' cause-related efforts are driven by business reasons just as not all brands' cause-related efforts are driven by social responsibility. It is important, however, to understand these benefits and their implications.

Marketing sense states and some research studies confirm that generally consumers would prefer buying a brand that is associated with a good cause than from other brands. In addition to loving the wonderful taste of Ben and Jerry's ice cream, the fact that the brand generously supports so many causes would probably be a strong reason for the brand being preferred by so many customers. The knowledge that a part of the money paid to a brand is going to a good cause adds to the positive emotional component of the brand. American Express launched a cause-related marketing programme in 1983 when they pledged to donate one cent towards the restoration of the Statue of Liberty on every transaction made to the card. There was a significant increase in new cards purchased as well as an increase in card usage.

In addition to boosting sales, cause-related brands can also charge a premium over competition. Often consumers do not mind paying a premium for a brand that is known to be generous to a well-known charity as consumers feel that the brand deserves the premium. Understandably there are many consumers who feel more comfortable in patronising cause-supporting brands rather than making actual donations of time or energy to the cause. Patagonia is a good example of a brand that uses premium pricing to capitalise on its cause-related brand equity.

Associations with a cause works towards reducing the negative connotations associated with the brand. Supporting a meaningful cause can do wonders for brands in terms of improving brand image and equity. Liquor and tobacco brands often associate themselves with causes as a means of negating a part of the disrepute associated with their industry. Unfortunately, some tobacco brands appear to be more involved in advertising their cause affiliation than actually supporting the cause, and the lack of intent shows up to work against them.

Brands that are seen to be possessing a very commercial and greedy image may wish to develop a softer image by showing a softer, nicer side by donating to charitable organisations.

Some use cause-related marketing to soften the greedy image attached to them for using cheap labour in Asian sweat shops.

Brands that plan to approach the money market for raising money from the public often show the warm side of their personality by publicly supporting charitable causes. Investors who are not doing extensive research on the brand may invest because they believe a brand with good intentions can be trusted.

Cause-related branding has a lot to offer brands and therefore this route is being used by many brands. There are several successful examples of cause-related branding working wonders for brands. However, it must be understood that a poorly developed cause strategy will lead to little or no benefits for the brand. The days when a brand could merely tie up with a well-known charity and earn brownie points are over and the intricacies involved in making cause-related branding work are worthy of careful consideration.

In branding, adopting a strategic perspective is critical. In cause-related branding it becomes even more critical as the process of establishing an association with a cause takes significant investment of time, effort and money. Reaping the benefits of the association takes time, and delinking from a cause can have strong negative repercussions for a brand. The involvement of the highest echelons of management is crucial in decisions involving cause-related branding. As a thumb rule, brands should have at least a three-year commitment to a cause before embarking on cause-related branding.

There are three levels of decisions that brands need to look at and the implications of each category of decisions is to be understood before planning for any kind of cause-related branding:

1. Deciding the category

There are a wide range of categories of causes ranging from care of deprived children to restoration of dignity of abused seniors. Categories are wide and can encompass a wide range of sub-categories. Within the cause category of care for senior citizens there are sub-categories addressing issues such as care for abandoned elders, medical treatment of deprived senior citizens, etc. It is important to choose the right kind of category and sub-category as a prelude to deciding a relevant issue to back within this category. While choosing a category brands can look for causes that have a strategic connection with the product line. Ganga, a soap brand, associated itself with the cause of cleaning the river Ganges with a part of its sales proceeds. This had tremendous relevance as the Ganges has great significance in India. It is believed that Ganges water will wash away one's sins. The Ganges also supplies water to many states in India. Cleaning the Ganges has both religious and practical significance.

2. Deciding the specific issue

Categories of causes comprise different issues. Issues are specific such as programmes to aid restoration of dignity of senior citizens who feel deprived of dignity due to their age. Focusing on specific issues is important for brands as it helps fine-tune the values that flow from the association.

3. Deciding the specific institutions

Unless the brand is willing to create a trust that handles the responsibilities of the cause, it will have to depend on institutions to run the operational aspects involved in the execution of cause-related activities. Aligning with an institution that caters to a specific cause can provide a brand with strong associations. An association with United Way can connote respect and concern for the elderly. However, brands need to ensure that they are not overshadowed by charities that are stronger brands than their sponsors.

Given below are some of the aspects that need to be studied before a brand decides to associate with a charitable cause.

1. What is the relevance of the cause to the brand's consumer segment?

Association with a charitable cause does not mean that consumers will automatically hold the brand in high esteem. Consumers must find the cause relevant to their value system before the brand receives any approbation. There are some causes that immediately strike a chord. ConAgra Foods, America's second largest food company that has over 80 household brands, launched Feeding Children Better, a huge corporate initiative dedicated to ending childhood hunger. This initiative did a lot to the brand as mothers related to the cause and warmed to it. But not all cause affiliations may work. For example, not all consumers may be equally supportive of a cause that looks at providing food and shelter to immigrants/refugees. These consumers may be more supportive of causes that benefit their own countrymen.

2. How different is it?

Many people are inured to causes, and even associations with a good cause like Cancer Care may neither draw much attention to the brand nor to the cause, nor would the association be very memorable. Finding a cause that is relevant and yet different would help in enhancing the memorability of the brand and cause. The Body Shop's efforts against animal testing and supporting sustainable development by sourcing ingredients and accessories from socially and economically marginalised producer communities is an 'exotic' cause that's different yet something that people can relate to easily.

3. Can the cause be owned?

It is normally difficult to own a cause as this would require immense investment of resources. Some brands end up virtually owning a cause like ConAgra owns the cause of ending childhood hunger. Patagonia has intertwined its business and cause activities. Patagonia has invested in the protection, restoration and maintenance of wildland ecosystems and biodiversity in the Patagonia region and will probably not see many other brands supporting this cause. The task of guarding the cause associations may not be very tough given its niche nature.

4. Will it hold enduring relevance with this segment?

Some causes are contextual. These causes appear to touch a sensitive chord with consumers and then suddenly seem to lose their appeal. Often charities in the Third-World countries catering to cyclone victims suddenly find their support waning in the wake of a fresh new tragedy in a different part of the country. Public sympathy often veers towards the more recent tragedies.

5. How will the relationship be positioned?

The nature of the brand's relationship with the cause can

influence consumer perceptions of the brand. A brand should contribute more than money to a cause. Investing time and talent too adds to the credibility of the brand's support to the cause. Brands that appear to only offer financial support may be seen as 'forced' or not completely committed, and this could in some cases prove counterproductive.

6. Controversial issues

Brands need to be careful while handling causes associated with controversial issues. For example, a 'euthanasia' support foundation campaigning for change in legislation towards euthanasia may be seen by some as a worthy cause but association with this cause may lead to the brand supporting it being embroiled in controversy at some stage of its association if public opinion suffers from the occasional mood swing. While some brands court controversy through short-term associations with controversial causes, this could be risky as well as counterproductive as the issue could turn ugly and taint the brand.

Cause-related branding works best when it is driven by the core values of the brand. Like anything else that is forced, cause-related branding could prove counterproductive if it is not a 'natural' facet of the brand. When it is not 'natural' to the brand, the cause-related activities are de-prioritised and lose focus often with a corresponding effect on the brand. Some organisations such as GE encourage their employees to participate in supporting causes. The Elfun Society is a global organisation of GE volunteers that supports causes by providing much needed time, energy and expertise and this adds credibility to GE as these activities flow naturally from the brand.

In an increasingly cynical world, the value of genuinely sensitive acts is extremely high. There are several cries for brands to show greater responsibility and to share a small part of their wealth with the less privileged. The current economic strife created by schizophrenic brands that show dissonance between their different actions has led to lower levels of consumer belief in brands. Cause-related branding performed with genuine intent can help restore consumer trust and build brand equity.

6

The Celebrity As a Brand

CELEBRITIES can be brands if they plan their life well. Some celebrities are brands and have an enduring value while others fade into oblivion over time. There are celebrities in all walks of life – game show hosts, politicians, film stars, sportspersons – to mention a few. Many celebrities have reputation managers whose job is to build the celebrity as a brand. However, most reputation managers seem to view this task as one of getting the celebrity as many sponsorship contracts as possible and ensuring that the celebrity enjoys favourable media coverage through a combination of good PR and tactical behavioural displays.

The assumption appears to be (and it is not always wrong) that stardom has a limited life span and one should cash in on it to the best of one's abilities. Celebrities can make themselves enduring brands. A long relationship with their audience has tremendous commercial potential. It is important that the 15 minutes of fame is leveraged to create an enduring relationship.

The nature of the relationship that the celebrity has with his/her audiences gives cues for how the brand relationship can be developed. The nature of the relationship also gives an indication of the kind of duration of the relationship. Louis L'Amour probably had a relationship with his reading audiences as a realistic link with the excitement of the Wild West. A relationship like the one that Louis L'Amour had with his readers could be extended for decades together through the creation of Western cowboy theme cities, adventure resorts, etc.

The Beatles had a great relationship with their audience based on fresh sound and a refreshingly cheeky attitude to life. This relationship has lasted for over four decades. As the group, their music and interests evolved, they remained relevant to their audience who were also evolving and had changing needs.

Importantly, their timing was perfect. They caught a generation on the upswing and grew with them. Even recently when a collection of The Beatles number one hits was released, it was a hit probably indicating that their ageing fans still loved their music.

Celebrities must keep in mind the changing needs of the audience in order to remain relevant to their audience. Madonna has been extremely successful in reinventing herself over time to remain a vibrant brand over time. From a 'material girl' to someone who has developed a spiritual side, Madonna has changed the rules of the game several times over, each time providing her fans with a new facet of her personality to appreciate her for. Madonna's enormous musical talent has helped her stay relevant musically which is her core relationship with her audience. Madonna keeps adding to her offerings through new ventures like her book of children's stories.

Relationships should not remain stagnant and need to evolve over time. Bob Dylan did nothing to let his relationship with his audience evolve and so he remains confined to his generation with only nostalgic memories remaining. Despite being seen as a musical lightweight, Britney Spears has become a huge name in the entertainment business. She started with a cute-young-girl image and slowly changed her image to that of a sexy young woman with her kiss with Madonna at the MTV music awards showing her to have 'grown up'.

Brands are driven by values and these values can be leveraged for new opportunities If Ivan Lendl's relationship with his audience was based on his achievements through physical fitness, he could probably drive this relationship by endorsing fitness programmes, diets and fitness related clubs that remind and reinforce the values that defined him and brought him success.

A lot of celebrities do things that are not in line with their relationship with their audience, seemingly in attempts to get into the limelight. Justin Timberlake tearing Janet Jackson's blouse during the Super Bowl break was seen as a desperate attempt to add newsworthiness to their image and probably did more to harm their equity than add to it. Britney Spears's marriage has been touted as a desperate publicity stunt.

Differentiation is the cornerstone of success for any brand. The famous Yorkshire and England cricketer Geoffery Boycott has always been known for his frank, analytical and no-nonsense comments. This attribute gave him the opportunity to become a respected cricket commentator after his playing days were over. His honest and at times vitriolic comments have set him apart from milder, more apologetic counterparts and made him a much sought-after commentator with a large number of admirers.

UK blues guitarist Eric Clapton, a cult figure in the early 1970s for his distinctive style of guitar work, has over the years been able to create an unparalelled niche in the world of music. Over 30 years after he came into to the limelight, Clapton continues to enjoy immense following.

Celebrity brands often are inspirational and this can be a great advantage to the celebrity. There are many who would love to be as talented as Serena Williams or as talented and beautiful as Steffi Graf or have as great musical abilities as Mark Knopfler. Some brands that identify the feeling of 'I wish I could be like them' and make the most of it. There are many ways this can be done, from talks to books or by just creating a mystique around their persona.

But it is important to maintain integrity at all times for it is tough for a brand to successfully live a double life. In organisation brands it is relatively easier, but in celebrity brands it is far tougher as the truth will come out sooner or later and erode the equity the brand has built over time.

Celebrity brands must try developing values/facets that are natural to them. Princess Diana was extremely natural and this was core to her personality. She probably never cared about personal brand building or reputation management, but her relationship with people across the world shows that she was one of the most popular celebrities of modern times and a powerful brand. Her remarkable life has shown dramatic ups and downs, widely varying characteristics, but her greatest strength was her naturalness in all that she did.

Not every celebrity is a brand. Not every brand exploits its commercial potential to the fullest. Branding is for those celebrities who have the discipline, intent and energy to develop an honest relationship over time.

7

Internal Branding

EMPLOYEES are a very important audience for any brand. Unfortunately, few brands realise this though many brands hold forth about the importance of employees to the performance of the brand. No brand or organisation can function without people, but few brands know how to use branding to attract and retain the right kind of people.

Brands need good people. Most big brands do not have to struggle too much to attract good talent as the brand's name draws a lot of high-quality talent. Many people are willing to work for a good brand at a lower salary than they would get in a less -known company. Many of the world's top brands pay low salaries compared to their relatively smaller and far more aggressive competitors. They can get away with this because often many employees prefer the stability and solidity of a large company and enjoy the reflected glory of working for a famous brand rather than working at a higher salary for a less-known brand. Brand building amongst existing and prospective employees can depress costs, increase productivity and strengthen brand equity not just with existing and prospective employees but with the general public as well.

These are a few ways to use your brand to attract and retain employees.

Communicate the brand's intent with clarity

A brand's intent is about what the brand wants to do. For any brand to do well, it needs people who understand the brand's intent and relate to it. These people provide impetus to the brand because they believe in the brand mission.

Brands that communicate their intent with clarity can attract people who relate to the intent and want to partner the brand. These employees would probably not only stay with the organisation longer than the average employee but would also probably put more into their performance. They would provide the passion and aggression that any brand requires for success and growth. South West Airlines's strongly motivated team has been the backbone of their success, bailing them out of tight situations and responding with enthusiasm every time the brand had a problem.

Employees who relate to the brand's intent/mission are able to drive the brand more because they relate the brand's cause to their own cause and therefore are personally motivated to achieve the brands objectives. The average motivation level of many employees of non-profits is very high because of the sense of purpose that the brand provides. This sense of purpose often helps employees reconcile themselves to a lower salary and tougher working conditions. Many Internet start-ups were characterised by the strong sense of purpose provided by their organisation. Employees battled several problems because they felt that the brand they were working for was doing something revolutionary and they wanted to be a part of the revolution.

Research indicates that it is getting tougher to find brands where most of the employees wholeheartedly believe in the brand's mission and relate to it as keenly as they do with their personal mission. WalMart seems to be a good example of a brand where there are a significant percentage of employees who relate to the brand's intent strongly.

Aligning people with brand values

Brands stand for a set of brand values. All that they do must work to establish and reinforce these values whether the values are manifested through product features/benefits or customer service. Understanding the brand values and identifying people who are in sync with these values for each function is important.

If a brand's values are warmth and customer-friendly service, then it would be ideal to put people who are genuinely warm and friendly to man positions where there is customer interaction. A cold and efficient person may do a given customer service task equally efficiently. But in that case either the employee would be not representing the brand values according to customer expectations, or the employee would not be behaving naturally. Over a period of time such employees may find it stressful to continuously behave in a manner that is contrary to their nature and end up leaving the job. Either option is sub optimal for the brand.

If HR can align employees with brand values so that the employee is attitudinally inclined towards living that value, it would be better for the brand as employees would probably stay longer, do a better job, and the brand values would be reinforced and brand equity, strengthened.

Employees who are attitudinally inclined to be helpful would probably fit into the front end of customer care while those who are more inclined towards corresponding could handle back-end customer care such as replies to customer emails.

Drive that brand name

Many brands do not believe in being high profile, they do not see any reason to feature prominently in the news or do any high-power advertising. These brands are missing out a key insight – employees often develop a great amount of self-worth from the brand they are associated with. Many people feel that working for a good brand indicates their status in life. For them it is important to be known to be working for a good brand.

A large public sector organisation in India launched a huge high-visibility ad campaign that ran for three years across India. The objective was to make the brand extremely high profile and develop pride of association amongst employees. Employees suddenly found their company being portrayed as an extremely professional progressive organisation and found their own personal stature growing by association. Productivity and quality standards improved as the employees of the organisation lived up to the image communicated by the brand.

Differentiate always

In order to attract and retain the best talent, brands must look at differentiating themselves from other brands. The nature of differentiation would vary based on the kind of employees required. IT companies may want out-of-the-box thinkers, while an accounting firm may prefer straight-thinking, diligent and focused professionals. Apple may find it easier to get the kind of engineers with an innovative streak in them more easily than other computer brands because of the strong differentiated image that Apple has developed over the years.

Brand culture

Brand culture is about how an organisation operates. Brand

culture is the way the people working for a brand work together – their level of camaraderie, their team spirit, the ease with which they interact with each other, the rituals they follow. Brand culture is depicted in many ways from the passion the team feels for the brand to the free flow of information to whether the team eats their lunch together. South West, Apple and Levis are known for their great brand culture and this attracts many people to join these brands.

Treat them fairly

Brands that have a reputation for fair play tend to have a more stable and committed work force. Employees can work knowing that they will be treated fairly – this removes the need to constantly monitor one's behaviour for political correctness and enables employees to focus on their work and deliver good results. The reputation for fair play is powerful means of attracting and retaining talent – possibly a strong indicator of the state of affairs in many corporates.

Concern

Employers who are known to have concern for their employees would be able to retain employees longer. Knowing that one is working for an employer who will take care of one's interests tends to bring out the best of an employee and the brand is rewarded with good performance. Pfizer Inc. emphasizes "respect for people" as its employer-branding position with a child-care centre at their headquarters, which reflects the company's commitment to help out its employees with sick children.

Concern shown for the employees builds the credibility of the brand. If a brand does not display concern for its own employees, would it be seen as having concern for its consumers? The other benefit is the positive word of mouth that the employees spread among consumers.

Employees need to see the good side of the brand before they can pass on the good word to the consumer. Brand building truly starts with the employees.

8

How Does Advocacy Work for Brands?

IT has been recognised by marketers the world over that the best form of advertising is the recommendation of a brand by satisfied customers. Marketers have realised that brand advocacy can create immense savings as it would largely reduce the cost of acquiring new customers, a cost that constitutes a large portion of the marketing budget.

Many brands are trying to build advocacy through different means such as customer meetings, loyalty programmes, etc. with varying levels of success. Often one finds that there is no sustained programme for building advocacy because of the lack of a clear understanding of the factors that drive advocacy. This is not that people don't want to talk about brands. Often enough customers like to recommend brands as a means of displaying their knowledge as well as to help others. Discussions on brands and brand experiences often feature in general conversations.

Advocacy is inextricably linked with the clarity of the brand promise and the brand's ability to deliver on this promise. Customers need to buy a brand with a clear understanding of what the brand is offering as this gives perspective to their expectations and consequently enhances their satisfaction levels. The more the satisfaction, the more positive the advocacy.

When a brand does not articulate its brand promise with clarity, consumers buy the brand for the wrong reasons. Sometimes a brand may deliver well, but still have unsatisfied customers. This is because the brand delivered not what the customer expected. This can lend to negative word of mouth.

Performance too is critical to building advocacy. Brands need to deliver on their brand promise without exception or incur the wrath of their consumers. Brands that are trying to grow on the basis of advocacy need to focus on delivering on their brand promise impeccably.

Advocacy is a complex process that is impacted by multiple factors. However, there are two key factors that drive advocacy.

a. The level of involvement that the consumer has with the brand.

b. The customer's level of satisfaction with the brand performance.

There is a close relationship between the advocacy level displayed and satisfaction/involvement levels of customers. At different satisfaction/involvement levels customers exhibit different degrees of advocacy from being aggressively supportive of the brand to being extremely deprecatory towards the brand.

The table on the next page illustrates the varying levels of advocacy at different combinations of satisfaction and involvement.

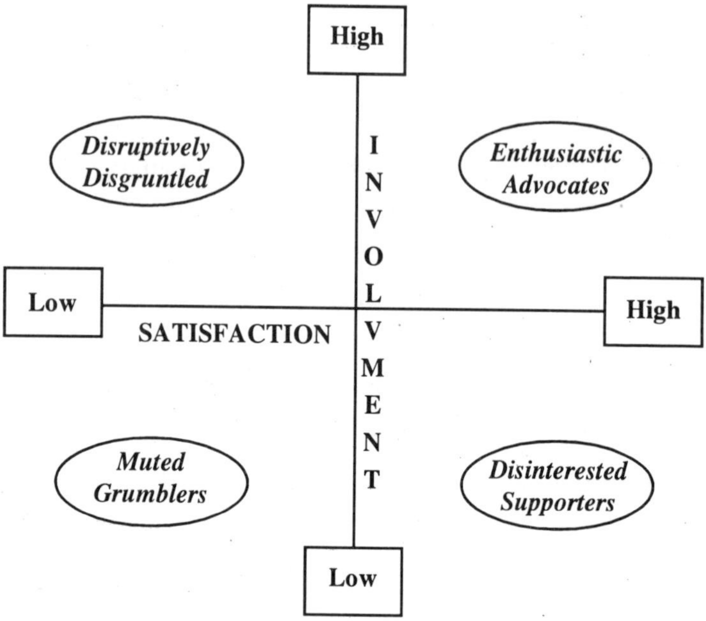

Muted grumblers

They are dissatisfied with the performance of the brand, but the involvement level is low. So expression of their unhappiness is not stated very often unless prompted. The average person would not make a hue and cry about a roll of defective sand paper or a packet of flimsy tissue papers.

Disinterested supporters

They may recommend a brand, but more often than not would do so in a grudging manner with the recommendation made only when prompted. Many people are not enthusiastic about their lighting at home even though they may use the very best of bulb brands and the performance may be extremely good. For that matter, not too many people actively recommend brands of ear buds !

Disruptively disgruntled

A nightmare for brands, this group can create havoc for a brand. These customers have high involvement, and when they are dissatisfied, they express their dissatisfaction without pulling any punches. A passionate motorcyclist who has bought a poorly-performing motorcycle would be disruptively disgruntled and spew negatives about the brand as its poor performance cuts him/her to the heart.

Enthusiastic advocates

This segment is every marketing manager's dream come true. The larger this base, the more robust the brand equity and the potential for sales. The average Harley Davidson customer, the average youngster visiting Disneyland and the average Snap On tools customer are enthusiastic advocates of these brands because of the high level of involvement they have with them and the high level of satisfaction that these brands deliver.

Impact of advocacy on the bottomline

Brand managers want customers to move up the advocacy ladder. While it may not be possible, it would be ideal for a brand to have all its customers as 'enthusiastic advocates'. Every movement up the advocacy ladder has a strong impact on bottomline and earnings. A reduction in the number of 'disruptively disgruntled' customers eases the load on the customer-care department, reduces the cost of freebies/ discounts given to pacify customers, reduces the number of customers lost through negative word of mouth, etc.

Different studies have shown that the cost of acquiring customers is calculated to be six times that of retaining a customer. When delighted customers actually bring in other customers without any cost to the brand simply on the basis of their positive word of mouth, the impact on the profitability of the brand is significant.

Brands need to look at their customers and understand how many of them feature in the different advocacy clusters. The change in the composition of these clusters can significantly impact profitability, brand equity and future sales.

Moving customers up the advocacy ladder

By influencing customers' involvement and satisfaction levels a brand will be able to move customers up the advocacy ladder. Increasing involvement without increasing satisfaction can lead to customers being vociferous in opposition of the brand. Enhancing satisfaction without building involvement will reduce vocal dissatisfaction but will not help in building powerful advocacy for the brand.

Brands that want to build advocacy must examine the brand to see whether they are delivering 'advocable' satisfaction. Understanding the factors that lead to advocacy of their brand will help them understand which specific features of delivery they need to focus on to create a disproportionate level of advocacy. For example, a supermarket may be very popular because of the speed of its checkout. Focusing on this particular aspect will increase advocacy levels for this brand rather than large-scale measures done in other aspects of the brand's performance.

Deterrents to advocacy

While moving customers up the advocacy ladder, brand managers must take into consideration two significant interrelated aspects that influence the customers' willingness to advocate a brand. These aspects are often offshoots of high involvement levels amongst customers for a particular brand. These aspects are:

a. The risk involved in advocating a brand and
b. The knowledge levels of the customer.

The risk involved in advocating a brand

The probable risk involved in advocating a brand is what often deters customers. The average man on the street is less likely to recommend an investment brand of mutual funds or a high-powered diabetes tablet as he would a brand of apparel. This is because of the fear that a recommendation that goes wrong can cause immense harm to the referee and the referrer would not want to be held responsible for that harm.

The knowledge levels of the customer

The product knowledge levels of the person recommending the brand come into play while advocating a brand. A person who does not know much about bikes would probably not venture to advocate a motorcycle brand. The lower the knowledge levels, often the lower the confidence levels to advocate a brand.

Overcoming these deterrents

To overcome these deterrents brands must try to educate consumers about their brands. The more the consumer knows about the brand and what makes it deliver superior performance, the greater the chances of the customer recommending the brand to others. Information on the rigour of the product testing, the superiority of the technology used, experts who endorse the brand, celebrities who use the brand, all work towards increasing involvement levels and building knowledge-based confidence that works to the brand's advantage.

This education also works towards building the brand's equity by establishing the brand's differentiation from competition and its relevance to the consumer. Relevance and differentiation are critical components of brand equity. Brand equity is an important factor in inducing advocacy as it provides connotations of the product/service's consistency and quality. Consistency and quality are necessary aspects for any brand that expects advocacy. This is especially true in the case of service brands where quality and consistency of delivery are tougher to maintain and where a bad experience is not forgotten or forgiven easily.

Complex as it may be, brands must look at building brand advocacy as an offshoot of the brand equity. Branding is a business process, and advocacy is a wise business tool.

9

Branding for Non-Profits

MANY non-profits like the Red Cross, United Way and CRY are strong brands. Many more non-profits have the potential to become strong brands but for the fact that they do not try to use the basic principles of branding. While this is often because of ignorance of branding, it is also due to the fundamental philosophy in many non-profits, that they are above branding and that branding requires large advertising budgets.

This is a flawed viewpoint for two reasons. Firstly, branding is not so much a marketing process these days as much as an organisational process. Secondly, branding benefits any organisation that has a strong intent and a clear-cut mission. For what purpose the organisation tries to generate a surplus (which is the difference between a profit and non-profit) is irrelevant to branding.

There is a popular notion that branding is all about high-powered advertising and involves big money. Many non-profit organisation do not consider active branding for lack of resources. Branding, however, can be of great use to non-profits for the very reason that many non-profits shun branding. The scarcity of resources makes branding extremely important because this will help in increasing revenue and depressing costs.

Branding helps marketing both in generating sales for the brand's products or services and in getting funds through donations and sponsorships. Today with several non-profits competing with each other for donations and sponsorship, the importance of branding in creating a competitive edge cannot be overlooked. The combination of the internal and external benefits of branding makes it an extremely relevant tool for non-profits.

Probably the greatest advantage that branding provides non-profits is focus and direction. It is important for any organisation to know exactly what it stands for and therefore what activities it should focus on. Often non-profits are not focused, as they believe that they are pursuing a worthy cause, and as long as the cause is worthy its boundaries are not important. Even a brand as popular as UNICEF found that its constituents were not clear of what it stood for and embarked on a branding exercise to revise and define its brand and communicate clearly to all its constituents what the brand stood for.

The process of branding forces one to define the brand promise and consequently the activities involved in living up to this promise. While focus helps in all aspects of an organisation's activities, the greatest advantage of focusing is channelling the energy of the non-profits team – employees and volunteers. The greatest advantage of most non-profits is the high enthusiasm and energy of their teams. Channelling this energy is critical. There's a lot that a motivated team can do. Greenpeace members' efforts of chaining themselves to railway tracks carrying nuclear waste cargo, cutting off ships to intercept whalers, and blocking waste discharge pipes in open water sources show their commitment to the cause of a clean environment. This springs from a deep appreciation of the brand mission.

Having defined what exactly its brand stands for, non-profit organisations should work on emphasising their differentiation from other non-profits. A well-differentiated brand is more noticeable and memorable – that makes people prefer this brand to any other. Often non-profits do not spell out the difference between their offering and other brand offerings, as they don't realise that the brand differentiation that is so obvious to them is not obvious to others. It is important for a volunteer of World Wildlife Fund to be clear about how the brand is different from Greenpeace or Friends of the Earth.

Non-profits that have a clear brand promise and explicitly defined values will find it easier than those that have vague brand promises and uncertain values. These non-profis can raise funds more easily because there will always be potential sponsors whose values match the brand's. The closer the match of the non-profit's brand values with the sponsor's brand values, the more beneficial the relationship can be for the sponsoring brand. This kind of brand– sponsor relationship is more desirable.

Non-profits often are guilty of not communicating effectively the relevance of what they are doing to their constituents. Consequently, many non-profits are seen as 'just another social institution' and do not earn the respect that they rightfully deserve. Only when a brand is respected and its relevance understood will customers, donors, etc. come forward to associate with the brand. Some non-profits are strident in communicating their relevance while others take it for granted that it is obvious to all that what they are doing is highly important and extremely relevant to society.

There is probably nothing as galling as buying/donating and being made to feel insignificant for not doing more. It is unfortunate, but many non-profits take the moral high ground because they are doing 'social service'. Looking down on customers and donors for not devoting themselves to the cause can be very damaging to the non-profit. Many non-profits make this mistake and lose out on repeat purchases and donations.

Branding is about creating a relationship with one's audiences. When non-profits are not transparent in their operations, they lose the involvement levels of their constituents. Constituents who pledge valuable resources often feel that they are not being included in crucial decisions taken by the non-profit on projects supported by these constituents. As a result they lose their enthusiasm for the project. Many a time constituents are not accepted wholeheartedly by the non-profit they are supporting, and consequently feel slighted. Often non-profits sideline sponsors and only involve them in money -related decisions. This will reduce their relationship with the donors/sponsors to only a financial relationship.

Many non-profits are not particularly known to be accountable. Sponsors and donors hesitate to contribute to such non-profits as they do not know whether the resources provided to the non-profit are being used in the manner planned or not. Many non-profits adopt a 'holier-than-thou' attitude when questioned about where and how funds donated were utilised and the results achieved. This attitude stands in the way of these non-profits getting repeat contributions from donors.

Non-profits that are accountable for the money received are more likely to get support not only in cash but also in kind as donors/sponsors know that their contribution is appreciated and being put to good use. Accountability is a key factor that impacts brand building for non-profits as it shows the brand has integrity and takes its brand promise seriously. A non-profit that is seen as not accountable will immediately be perceived as being wasteful, and that is a sin from a donor's point of view.

Non-profits need to take a good hard look at the way they are functioning and how they can improve their standing. Branding is the best tool for non-profits to survive and thrive in a competitive world. The biggest challenge for non-profits is to understand and embrace branding in its true spirit.

10

Building Nation Brands with Pride

AS THE global marketplace becomes more competitive, nations are now competing with each other as brands. Nations resort to branding for attracting tourists, increasing the desirability of exports, improving the ability to attract talent and bringing in foreign investment for business.

Probably the strongest nation brand is America, which for long has been able to do with ease what many nation brands aspire to do. America attracts tourists, investments and skilled high-quality manpower that are so crucial to a nation's economy. American products often get a premium in international markets because of their lineage. Exports from America are fairly high because of the value attached to the 'American' tag. The rapid ascendancy of America-the-brand has made many nations realise the need for nation branding. The growth of brand USA has lessons for all nations.

The nation-branding process is based on a complex long-term plan linked to the economic and social development of a nation. While some countries realise the need to do nation branding, others are merely aware of this need. Taiwan and other Asian countries are trying to build themselves as attractive hubs for low-cost manufacturing. Malaysia and Singapore are aggressive in their nation branding process and use advertising to drive tourism.

The Rainbow Nation has realised the importance of branding and is said to have followed the Unilever branding process to build brand South Africa. There has been a concerted effort to get internal processes in place to ensure that economic and social development goes hand in hand.

A challenging task of nation branding is developing a strong sense of pride amongst the people of the nation, and then using this pride to drive social and economic progress through a pre-defined path. The path could be tourism or low-cost manufacturing, or anything else the country has to offer. Often this reflects the intrinsic values and traditions of its people. Using native strengths for economic progress can be the key to success for many nations. To do this successfully one has to know the 'personality' of the nation as one would understand the personality of individuals.

Nations as agglomerations of human beings have the same characteristics as human beings. Some nations appear proud, while others have a sense of timidity as their most visible facet. National pride is natural to most people though it may be deeply suppressed due to situational constraints. A person who has grown up in abject poverty may at times find it difficult to feel national pride as the bitterness of their situation may taint their viewpoint.

National pride is critical for the economic growth of nations. Pride brings with it self-confidence and the courage to take risks critical to innovation and progress. Pride also brings with it high standards of delivery in different forms from workmanship, delivery schedules, quality parameters of goods produced, courtesy extended to tourists, honesty of government officials to even clean water and good roads.

Countries like Greece have a tremendous sense of national pride and heritage. Visitors to Greece are treated well, and there are hardly any instances of travellers having a bad experience with the people of Greece. In China it is matter of pride that government officials process foreign trade related documents extremely quickly with the minimum of bureaucracy or fuss. Singapore's standards of cleanliness and hygiene are admired across the world.

Pride comes from having a strong sense of national identity and a keen desire to maintain the national heritage. Pride gives the motivation to conduct oneself in a manner that will do the nation proud as well create products and services that are truly world class. This is manifested in several forms from courteous behaviour towards tourists, an absence of corruption, no littering, etc.

The state of Andhra Pradesh in India seems to have understood the complexity involved in place branding. What the state has learned can be successfully replicated by the nation brand India. The state had realised that it is difficult to build a sense of pride in people when their surroundings are far from ideal. The task began with widening of the roads, building flyovers to reduce traffic snarls and beautifying the state. The government also computerised government offices so that productivity improved and the citizens' experience of interacting with the government also improved leading to increased trust in the governments initiatives.

The government used technology extensively to track and eliminate problems such as pilferage of power. A system of decentralisation of decision-making was put in place to ensure local needs were looked into. However, accountability was strongly linked to authority. The government aggressively solicited investment and brought exciting projects to the state like the International School of Business, the Microsoft Institute, etc.

Big cities were not the only beneficiaries. Women in small villages have been taught to use the Internet as a means of getting the latest information on vegetable prices in towns, so that they can price their produce to get a better margin. There are several instances of such improvements percolating to the grassroots.

The results have been encouraging. There seems to be an increased sense of pride in the Andhra people who suddenly have a lot to boast about like good roads, a clean and green environment, projects of international fame – all based in their own state. The state's attractiveness as a business destination has seen employment increase, and correspondingly, standard of living has improved too. Reports of the improvement in the state has led to non-resident Indians of Andhra origin investing in Andhra Pradesh. Faced with a newfound improvement across different facets of life, Andhraites are taking more pride in themselves and are also becoming more demanding of the government, thus increasing efficiency and reducing corruption.

There is still a long way to go in the branding of Andhra Pradesh, but the effort is in the right direction. Growth has not only been economic but has seen social development of backward classes, minorities and the like. There are several sections of society and parts of the state that need to be worked on, but the movement has begun and there are lessons here for India the brand.

Governments working on nation-branding projects must try and ensure that there are enough programmes to stir national pride in their people. Governments must help preserve the heritage of their respective countries so that their people are able to look back on the past with pride and use this pride as a motivator and source of confidence for building the future. If need be, governments should educate their people about the nation's heritage.

If pride is not instilled in the people, the nation will only have the façade of being a brand. In such a case, quality, cleanliness, etc. will have to be enforced through punitive actions and not through voluntary natural behaviour from the citizens. This is not a sustainable exercise as it does not come from within.

Governments must also build on the examples set by its people as these examples serve as beacons of hope and reinforcement of pride for the nation at large. The sheer national pride of a football-crazy country that wins the World Cup can be overwhelming and the performance of a few individuals have the potential to lift a nation to higher levels of pride and delivery. Americans have always passionately celebrated their heroes, and this has led to tremendous pride, national unity and set aspirations amongst the public to be like their heroes.

Governments must encourage activities that build identity, unity and pride. Australia is a strong nation brand that sets a lot of value on traditions. Traditions link the past with the present and lead into the future. While many consider traditions old-fashioned, traditions are a powerful source of identity and reinforce the sense of pride one has in one's roots. Australians have a healthy sense of pride that probably gives them a competitive edge whether on the sports field or in the boardroom.

With pride comes resilience. Nations with a strong sense of pride have been able to bounce back after devastatingly tough periods. America, Japan, Germany and Britain are some examples of countries whose/in strong pride based on their glorious past gave them the motivation to re-attain their stature post the World War.

A nation with a sense of pride in itself tends to be a self-confident nation. Confidence is important for developing a vision and working towards that vision. The more confident the nation, the more daring and large the vision, and the greater the ability to drive the vision to reality. A confident nation is also one that can ideate, innovate and seize opportunities aggressively. This is evident in nations whose economies are doing well. These nations compete better not just because they can invest more but because of their willingness to think bigger and move more aggressively than others. Truly, nation-building is all about building confidence and pride.

11

Pharma Branding

MANY pharma brands today are in poor brand health. An industry that is assumed to have the good of mankind at heart has often proved to set commercial values higher than human values. The ensuing disillusionment in some audiences has affected pharma brands' credibility. The vast number of class-action suits filed show that pharma brands are not flawless. The lack of rigour and ethics in product testing by some brands and the unseemly haste in trying to rush new drugs into the market to cash in on them have taken away the sheen from many a pharma brand. If pharma brands ever needed branding to rescue their image, it is now.

Branding of pharma products or services requires immense rigour and a thorough knowledge of the principles of branding. Pharma branding starts from the corporate brand and mission. The corporate brand – its mission, vision, values, goals and processes – helps in creating credibility for individual brands, and the sum of the individual brands' equity adds back to the corporate brand. The corporate brand as an employer attracts and retains employees using its credibility and culture, and these employees create products and services in line with the mission, vision and values to further the brand's equity.

Some of the more evolved pharma brands have inspiring mission statements, and this sets the tone for the organisation's actions. Pfizer proclaims in its mission 'We dedicate ourselves to humanity's quest for longer, healthier, happier lives through innovation in pharmaceutical, consumer, and animal-health products.' GSB talks of its desire to improve the quality of human life by enabling people to do more, feel better and live longer. The results are there for all to see. These brands are able to attract high-quality researchers who enjoy doing what they are doing because this is in line with their personal values and because the organisation's culture makes them enjoy their work, and the results are high-quality products and services. These are brands that have a good intent and are clear about what they want to do.

It is important for corporate pharma brands to have missions that are inspiring and personalities that are liked. After all, many pharma companies make their money from people's sicknesses and often are seen by the negative-minded as preying on the sick. It is a simple matter of perception, but most brands manage it poorly with their other gaffes working against them. While doctors too make their living by curing sick people, doctors are liked because of their personal interaction, their knowledge and advice, their service in their patients' time of need. A simple tablet or capsule may do a lot more for the patient, but its lack of personality or friendliness makes it impersonal. (Some brands have figured out how to neutralise this to some extent by using different colours for their pills.)

There are further biases against pharma products revealed through a qualitative study. Pharma products remind their users of their frailty and mortality, and this is never a pleasant thought. The process of putting an unnatural substance into one's system is seen as unpleasant and undesirable. Except for some who glory in hypochondria and others who enjoy pill popping for the satisfaction of feeling that they are constantly being restored to peak health, the majority seem to dislike having to take medicines to be healthy. With many negative connotations associated with the pharma category, it is important for pharma brands to develop positive associations.

Unfortunately, many corporate pharma brands are seen as greedy and unscrupulous. Brands tend to have a limited time frame to cash in on their efforts once a new molecule is discovered and this haste probably hits them in the long run. Some brands lose equity because their words and actions don't match. Equity is eroded because of poor values and processes. Sometimes the haste to go to market leads to poor testing and the brand later gets hit with lawsuits. Sometimes it is the lack of proper testing policy that allows improper testing on animals or humans. This creates a lot of ill will against these brands. Some high-profile brands have been accused of improper testing procedures with allegations of them enrolling alcoholics and homeless people as test subjects by 'buying' volunteers who are in need of easy money.

The number of high-publicity lawsuits that have featured prominently in the media has done a lot of harm to the pharmaceutical industry. Whether these are law suits filed by customers against pharma companies or the public legal squabbling of rival companies over patents does not matter to the public who view these companies as low on values and ethics.

A recent survey indicates that there is a high degree of scepticism towards pharma companies' claims. This is probably leading to a greater number of people moving to alternative medicines because of their gentle curing properties that have no side effects. Homeopathy, ayurveda, acupuncture, etc. are gaining in importance as the world turns to time-tested deep-curing solutions.

There is probably a case for branding the process followed both for researching new products and testing them. The entire process then gets split into sub processes that become the guidelines for any such activity in the company. This pushes innovation and rigour to the forefront. The process is seen as scientific and rigorous and therefore builds the brand's credibility. This can also make for an enduring PR story that celebrates the brand's core values. By branding the process an additional brand property is created that resurfaces strongly every time a new product is launched. Importantly, this works in attracting high-quality talent which wants to become a part of this process.

Pharma brands would also do well in putting forth researchers who are projected as celebrities because of their association with the process and their role in developing and testing the product. Again this builds a human element, credibility and relevance and adds back to the equity of the process.

Corporate pharma brands build equity based on strong PR and communication support. Customers trust the brand name and their country's regulatory authorities' rigour and integrity when they consume a pharma product. This trust is huge as the customer is placing their life or health in the pharma companies' hands. In the case of doctors who find that they have been advocating drugs that are actually harmful for their customers, the sense of guilt and anger at betrayal can be very long lasting.

Pharma brands often complain that they are not able to get across to doctors (who form an important audience for them) enough. Doctors find the unending flood of information from pharma companies a necessary evil but often grudge the time they spend with medical representatives. This leads many pharma companies to try and bribe doctors for their time by giving them freebies. This reduces the process of interaction to a 'loveless' transaction. If their key audience views them with scepticism then these brands cannot go far.

Pharma companies that appeal to doctors both on a personal and professional level evolve a lasting relationship. The feeling that one is being recognised as an individual and not just as an important referral for business can help create genuine bonding. Glaxo demonstrated through their loyalty programme in India that professional respect for the doctor combined with recognition and appreciation of the doctor as an individual can lead to increased business and a strong lasting relationship.

Pharma brands can earn a lot of equity and deflect the image of being impersonal money-grabbers by genuinely involving themselves with cause-related activities. At one level these activities can be in line with the ailment that their drugs are aiming to prevent or cure. At another level they can be involved with a cause such as an institute that takes care of sick doctors, which shows that they genuinely care.

There are many pharma brands that don't live their values and this gives a great opportunity for new brands with heart and commitment to make a big mark in this industry.

12

The Role of Emotion in Branding

IT is strange that at a time when the world is passing through an emotionally arid phase brands have forgotten the benefits of using emotion to build and strengthen brand equity. The current scenario is largely bereft of emotion – one of the most potent weapons of brands for years. But there is a huge need for emotion as many people yearn for emotion in an increasingly sanitised and faceless world.

To understand the importance of brands to consumers, who form a part of society, it is important to understand the dynamics of society and consumers' participation in social life. Family is not the same as it was in the past. In many countries across the world, the joint family concept no longer exists wherein all members of the same family would live together under the same roof often with the oldest male member as the head of the family.

The creation of nuclear families where husband, wife and children live together has seen family sizes shrinking. The awareness of the economic benefits of small families and the need for privacy, amongst other reasons, led to the breakdown of the joint family system and to the rise of nuclear families. There is an increasing number of small families with double-income-no-kids (DINKs), single parents and divorcees than in the past. All this has contributed to a reduced amount of security and emotional support available from the family as an institution. The change in family structure has happened across the world though the speed of transformation of the social structure varies across countries and cultures.

While the changes in the family structure has had its impact on some adults in the form of a greater feeling of loneliness and insecurity, the impact of being raised in a single-parent family can be even stronger for children. These feelings are further reinforced by some public school systems where classes are overflowing with students and where there is little personal attention or recognition of students as individuals.

Social interaction too has changed over the last hundred years. There is a reduction in social feeling, and often people do not know their neighbours or other people living in their neighbourhood. This re-emphasises the feeling of 'being on one's own' which is fine for some but makes others feel lonely.

Simple feel-good factors also have been on the wane. Mom and Pop stores where the shopkeeper knew the customer by name and could engage in a conversation every time the customer visited the shop are now being replaced with supermarkets that are impersonal and faceless. In the US and other countries, many Mom and Pop stores have faded out and have been replaced by high-efficiency supermarkets high on choice but low on customer emotional content.

Large corporations see thousands of employees working together often without knowing many of their colleagues. A lot of employees feel unnoticed and lonely as they work with strangers in cold surroundings. With depressions, recessions and other economic catastrophes leading to mass retrenchments, the feeling of insecurity and the need to be recognised, respected, reached out to and comforted is increasing.

Mass marketing has helped reduce costs, but at the same time it has led to an increased consumer feeling of being a single impersonal statistic in the economic chain. Often customers are led to realise that they are just that – customers of an organisation, not flesh-and-blood human beings.

In many countries people are gravitating towards cities, as rural areas are unable to provide adequate gainful employment and attractions. Cities are more crowded but less personal, and the stifling feeling of being all alone in a crowd is increasing.

The need for recognition and company has manifested itself in several ways. In the pre-Internet days Lonely Hearts Clubs were in vogue. The advent of the Internet has seen total strangers chat intimately with each other, and Internet relationships are real and often as or more complex than many offline relationships. The emotional needs of individuals are real and the need for 'security blankets' has grown.

In short, life has seen a rapid change on several fronts leading to a lot of people feeling less secure, more desirous of emotional bonding and requiring company and recognition. In this scenario, branding can prove to be invaluable as it provides consumers emotional gratification, personalisation, recognition and expression that is important for many people.

To many people, brands have lost their physical form and only retain their ethereal form. Brands are symbols representing goodness, affluence, luxury, the American way of life, God, the right choice, etc. If brands can represent such a variety of values, then it can only be inferred that this is so because consumers are willing to accept these values packaged in the form of different products and services.

The willingness to accept these brands as symbols represents the consumers' psychological needs. The consumption or possession of these brands as a means of filling these emotional gaps or reinforcing beliefs indicates the consumers' the state of mind.

Brands that are consumed over a period of time develop a great emotional relationship with their consumers who value the good times that they have had while consuming the brand and associate these with the brand. People who grew up drinking Coke were distressed when Coca Cola withdrew Coke from the market to launch New Coke as this rudely cut them off from their memories. Cadbury's Dairy Milk chocolates have a special place in the hearts of those who have consumed these from their childhood.

Brands create a feeling of self-worth and distinction. People purchase brands like BMW because of the status that it provides. Sure it's got great engineering, but that's not the only reason why many people buy a BMW. Chivas Regal is a part of many rich people's bar because of the distinction it confers even if it is not their personal favourite drink. Similarly, Harley Davidson's motorcycles or accessories add masculinity to their consumers' self-image. Many a brand of deodorant, cologne, perfume, lingerie, car, motorcycle, shirt, trousers, shoes, etc. are bought because they are believed to add sexiness and persona to their consumers.

Brands create a feeling of fraternity in different ways. Consumers like to be a part of a select club or a distinguished few such as Gold cardholders. In other cases there are some who feel nice being part of a large special consumer family like Apple consumers do. Consumers feel good just about meeting other consumers of the same brand as in the case of

Harley Davidson. People who buy Snap On tools enjoy discussing their tools with other Snap On tool buyers.

People like to feel young, smart, sexy, mature, intelligent, knowledgeable, special, cultured and more, and there are brands that cater to every emotional need. Consuming these brands gives the consumer a sense of satisfaction as that particular emotional need has been appeased for the moment.

Brands whose customers have an emotional connection with the brand have different advantages. They have the equity to face a near-death experience and still roar back to life the way Harley Davidson did. Customers who feel strong emotion for the brand tend to be loyal to the brand and only need an excuse to support the brand. This is an unbeatable advantage as it ensures the brand a set amount of business and forgiveness for the occasional small foibles that brand management fall prey to. Brands with such emotional equity can live forever.

Emotion can help in enhancing profitability. BMW, Mercedes, Yves St Laurent and Mont Blanc are brands that can charge a huge premium that customers are willing to pay because the brand adds an emotional component that they want.

The pressures of the marketplace have seen an increase in the number of sales promotions over the last few years. This has largely been to thwart competition, fight recessionary sales dips and keep investors happy and jobs secure. The ends are good, but the means often undermine the brands running these sales promotions because these brands are teaching customers to choose between brands on the basis of a rational decision instead of giving customers stronger emotional reasons to prefer their brand. Often customers buy impulsively and rationalise their purchase decision later because of the emotional appeal. But if brands themselves teach customers to decide rationally, then the entire marketing process becomes a function of product features and pricing, and this is a losing move for brands at large drastically reducing profitability margins. Importantly, this will also keep customers emotionally starved, reduce brand preference and kill loyalty.

If consumers don't feel the emotional value of brands, then branding is in danger of losing its relevance. It would be ironic if, at a time when emotional gratification is required possibly more than earlier, branding were to lose its relevance due to brand custodians' inability to identify and provide through brands the emotional gratification that consumers need.

13

The How and Why of Heritage Branding

THE term 'heritage brands' is normally used in the context of tourism branding where a country tries to use its heritage to make itself appear an attractive tourist destination. But there are many brands that are not places that can be called 'heritage brands'

Probably the strongest brands are those that actually go on to become part of a national, social or cultural heritage. As time goes by, these brands (if they retain their relevance) become an integral part of the nation's social or cultural context and derive strong equity from this context.

Consider the example of Coke and its place in the evolution of America over the last century. In addition to being a symbol of America, Coke stands for much more. In the last 100 years when America evolved as a superpower, Coke has been a symbol of the imagery of America and the power of being the original one.

Coke has been a constant as a nation evolved carrying connotations of 'Americanness'. Coke was supplied to American marines in Vietnam as a link with the world back home. Coke commercials like 'I want to buy the world a Coke' have touched a chord and become a part of American folklore. It's not surprising that when Coke pulled out 'the real thing' in order to give 'New Coke' a better opportunity in the market, people were appalled, and Coke loyalists sponsored protest rallies and boycotted the brand. This move by Coke was probably the equivalent of desecrating a national monument.

As generations of Americans grew up drinking Coke in good times and bad, the brand has evolved to the status of becoming a heritage brand. For many there's a feeling of bonding in-built just in one's near and dear sitting together and drinking a Coke. While maintaining relevance and vibrancy will always remain critical to the brand's survival, the brand is so closely linked to the national, social and cultural heritage that its success is almost guaranteed.

McDonald's is not as old as Coke, but again it has a strong heritage element. The association with America is indisputable not just because of the experience of millions of American families consuming the brand over the years, but also because the manner in which McDonald's has touched the lives of millions of Americans. Some estimates put the number of Americans who have worked in McDonald's at over 10 million, and one in every fifteen Americans has worked in a McDonald's as their first job. As a result McDonald's is seen as a brand that is inextricably linked to people's good times and individual growth.

There are some who argue that Ford too is a heritage brand. The role of Ford in 'creating' an American middle class by paying good wages and making a car that is inexpensive enough for the middle class to own made Ford associated with the development and growth of America's favourite mode of transport – the car. Though Ford has struggled as a brand, there are many who see Ford as a symbol of the development of the American middle class in terms of transport and work.

Starbucks looks like a brand that will become a part of America's socio-cultural heritage in due course. Over time more and more people will realise that many a matter that will be recorded in America's social, political or cultural history have been discussed at Starbucks outlets. Whether it is the state of the economy or the horrific September 11 attack or the last episode of *Friends*, it is probably discussed at Starbucks, and this is where a lot of the nations most discussed topics are publicly shared. When the significance of Starbucks is realised, Starbucks too will be well on its way to becoming a heritage brand.

Brands that become heritage brands have a few advantages over other non-heritage brands that compete with them. The advantages are:

1. Creates an added differentiation

Heritage brands have an added differentiation as compared to other brands. McDonald's not only is a respected eatery but for many Americans it also has an element of nostalgia as a place where they or their relatives and friends worked as a first job. While Burger King, Wendy's and In and Out may have been the first job for many an American, the numbers are stacked far higher in McDonald's favour, and this differentiation gives McDonald's greater memorability.

2. Creates a differentiation that gets stronger with time

The McDonald's advantage will only get stronger with time if it continues to be a preferred choice for youngsters as their first job. Similarly, the longer Coke is in existence, the stronger will be its image as a symbol of the growth and evolution of America, making the differentiation stronger over time.

3. Creates an added reason to consume

The reasons why a brand is consumed vary depending on the specific consumer context. It could be price, taste, associations, availability, occasion, etc. Heritage gives consumers one more reason to consume the brand. The nostalgia one feels at a McDonald's because one has worked there at some point of time is a strong reason why many an American would visit a McDonald's.

4. Loyalty abounds

There are many who share a deep relationship with heritage brands. For these people the brand is an integral part of their lives, and in some cases they see the failure of the brand as the loss of something precious to them. For some there is a sense of gratitude and loyalty towards these brands. These people could be former employees or the family of former employees, vendors, long-standing investors who have benefited from the association or consumers whose self-concept is tied up with the brand. This loyalty may pay off if the brand falls on hard times.

Most brands would want to become heritage brands and get the added stature and equity from this. This is not always possible as heritage brands have some well-defined features. Heritage brands tend to be mass based, so a large number of people need to be able to experience the brand and develop a relationship with it. McDonald's, Coke, Ford, Starbucks, Wal-Mart all have a widespread presence across their parent country enabling them to forge a relationship with people across the country leading to a commonality of feeling. The frequency of brand experience needs to be high for the feeling that the relationship has evolved and matured over time to sink in quickly and for the heritage association to set in. Importantly, the brand constituents must feel an emotional connect with the brand.

A constituent may not have an emotional connect with McDonald's purely as a consumer, but the connect may arise as a result of the constituent seeing McDonald's as the first step in the constituents career. Brands that want to evolve into heritage brands must sense the connect which often may not be obvious to marketing eyes but more from an overall brand perspective. Determining whether the nature of connect is desirable and assessing its overall impact on the brand in the long run are important.

If it is felt that the emotional connect can be built on and that this will help in the long run, then the brand needs to identify the drivers of this connect (which may not be linked with the marketing message of the brand) and use these to build on the heritage facet of the brand. This could be done in subtle ways such as focusing on hiring primarily inexperienced youngsters and letting them experience their first job in McDonald's as a means of building lifelong loyalty. Coke could probably create an online or offline production which shows America over the years with a Coke by its side. The avenues are many, but in all cases it is important to let the connect develop naturally and then subtly remind constituents of it so that the reminder and reinforcement is accepted and believed naturally.

Heritage brands can very quickly become old fuddy-duddy brands if they do not evolve with their audience. McDonald's is currently a beleaguered brand that is struggling with competition and trying to maintain relevance with its audience. Heritage is of little use to brands that are not well managed. Heritage can be a powerful benefit but if the core of the brand is dying and the brand's emotional connect with its audiences is lacking, then heritage will not save the brand.

The benefits of heritage brands are many. The potential to get better as they get older is a powerful benefit. Brands need to look at how fast they can make themselves 'heritage' brands and let time strengthen this unique competitive advantage for them.

14

What Investors Should Know about Branding

BRANDING is the strongest driver of business value in organisations today. Given that branding today represents an organisational process for value creation, an understanding of branding is important for investors these days.

A simple example here would serve the purpose of demonstrating the relationship between branding and the creation of value. The world's largest brand Coke has been valued at $70 billion. What is this value? Is it the cost of inventory, assets, etc?

This value, called by accountants as goodwill and brand people as the brand's valuation, is a monetary value attached to the brand as an asset. It is based on the several factors that drive brand equity. This is the sum of the value that millions of individual consumers have in their mind for the brand. It is the value of preference that one brand possesses over others. It is the value of the premium that a brand can command over competition. It is the value of all the associations that consumers have with a brand that results in higher sales. It signifies the potential business that the brand can expect from customers in the future.

Investors need to be concerned about the brand equity of the brands they have invested in. Brand equity helps brands deliver consistency in achieving high sales volumes and earn greater revenue for the brand. Consistently high sales volumes also help in suppressing costs as the economies of scale come into play. Brand equity helps a brand charge a premium over a comparable product offering from other lesser-known brands to get a higher per unit realisation.

A brand with strong equity can get a higher realisation on their marketing budget as it takes less to remain top of mind with consumers where a relationship exists. Consumers respond more readily to a known brand's communication than an unknown offering. Consumers are more willing to try out new offerings from a strong brand, and this significantly reduces the cost of new product launches.

The ease of adding on new distribution channels is also greater in the case of strong brands. Trade is often willing to stock new offerings from powerful brands, and in many cases even accept lower margins as compared to lesser-known brands.

Strong brands are able to attract and retain high-quality talent with ease. Often employees are willing to work for a large brand for a lower salary than they would get elsewhere. For example there are many smaller companies that offer better salaries than the mighty Microsoft. Good brands also benefit with a stable workforce. A study indicates that employees of well-known brands work with the same company for more years than people who work for lesser-known brands. IBM and P&G are known for having long-standing loyal employees.

Branding depresses costs, drives volumes, earns higher realisation per unit and provides stability to company performance. Obviously, branding fulfils all the parameters that an investor would look forward to. In addition it must be noted that strong brands also tend to have reasonably sound share prices that remain relatively stable. Strong brands tend to outperform the stock market index and deliver good returns.

Investors can make or break brands. Often promoters are reluctant to go public because of the fear of losing control over their brand. This is a realistic fear for as long as they control the brand they can support the brand intent which is their intent too. Sam Walton's dislike of the thought of taking Wal-Mart public is well known. Maintaining the purity of intent helps the brand focus and get stronger over time leading to all the benefits mentioned above. The entry of other investors can lead to the pursuit of returns at the expense of intent and from there the brand edifice can start to crumble.

Often investors do not concern themselves with branding. Their incessant demands for greater returns from the brands they have invested in often leads to brands getting into frequent sales promotions that can actually erode the very brand equity that delivers so many benefits to the brand. Frequent discounting, one-for-one offers, etc. lead consumers to mentally downgrade the brand, thereby reducing the possibility of the brand earning a premium.

Investors need to realise that brand equity is the goose that lays golden eggs, and therefore it is in their own interest to sustain brand equity rather than erode it for short-term gains. It is said that the American car industry never developed enough brand equity to fight the Japanese car brands because the Americans were more focused on delivering returns to investors than building brand equity, while the Japanese, who chose bank loans as their mode of financing, did not have investor pressure and could focus on building brand equity. The results of this myopic perspective speak for themselves as Japanese cars rule the American market.

Brands that mortgage their future for the present deliver healthy dividends while also rapidly diminishing stock value.

The dividends often may not compensate for the drop in stock value over time.

Investors should play a proactive role in the brands they have invested in by making sure that these brands invest in brand-building programmes. It is important for them to understand the key drivers of brand equity and ensure that nothing is done that negatively impacts these drivers. For example, in the case of a fashion brand it would probably be wiser to invest in a branding programme that builds the brand's image of fashion rather than invest the same money in machinery that will deliver lower costs. Understanding the need to boost bottomline by creating a greater premium rather than by saving on production is the difference that these investors would need to recognise.

Understanding the vision of the brand will enable investors provide wise guidance for the organisation and get the best returns on their investment. The investors in Apple were a wise lot who understood what the brand's vision and potential were and helped the brand by sanctioning investment in areas where the brand needed support and in areas that actually drove the brand's performance.

Investors need to know the state of the industry in which the brand is operating so that they know what to expect from the brand and where the brand can reach. The early investors in Apple were visionaries and recognised the potential of the brand. They were willing to invest huge amounts of money in advertising the brand and had faith that the market would repay their confidence as it did.

Investors are a myriad mix of people ranging from the avaricious to the needy. Investors need to be educated about the brands they have a stake in so that their decisions and expectations are tempered with reality and knowledge rather than a single-minded obsession to get the maximum return at the cost of all else. Few brands take the effort of explaining the brand situation to investors and hence investors tend to exert as much pressure as possible to see huge results. As more and more brands stand up and educate their investors properly, there will be an increasing appreciation amongst investors of the reasons why some brand custodians take unpopular decisions in the interests of the brand.

Top management who can educate the investors and take a stance are few. The plummeting performance of brands during the recent recession will probably have brought through the realisation that brand equity is an organisation's single most powerful tool and needs to be protected for the investors' investment to deliver good returns. Hopefully, this realisation will lead to better days both for brands and investors.

15

The Branding of Political Parties

POLITICAL parties have been known for their astute use of marketing tools from advertising to PR and have displayed a keen understanding of marketing concepts like positioning. Indeed political parties and politicians often reposition opponents with devastating results. Political parties have for long been using a few principles of branding to strengthen their relationship with their constituents. Now, more political parties are wholeheartedly adopting branding to strengthen every aspect of their being.

Political parties are important to manage the process of democratic selection. However, each party has to prove its relevance to its constituents to earn votes. Political parties represent a stand on different issues important to voters and a distinct set of values, and voters gravitate towards the party that seems to best represent their interests on different issues.

Political parties use branding to build focus, depict the values they stand for and build a relationship with their audiences whether these are workers, the electorate, the media or anyone else. The Democrats and Republicans in America both are said to have used branding extensively to build vibrancy in their relationship with their constituents. This relationship presumably would be a means of soliciting votes, donations, media coverage, etc.

In the United Kingdom, the Labour Party presumably rebranded itself as New Labour to depict modern values and cast off the old image of a party whose stint in power was associated with union problems. New Labour was an attempt to connote a new sense of purpose and vibrancy.

The principles of branding are as relevant for political parties as they are in the branding of any consumer service though the branding process may vary.

As in the case of other categories that seek to use branding, the vision of the party is critical to the success of the party. Political parties attract workers and votes on the basis of their vision and values. As the party's constituents associate their future with the party's ability to translate the party's vision into reality, the vision becomes an important factor in determining the party's relevance to its audience. In political branding there is no tangible product, and therefore the quality of vision, the relevance of the vision and the party's ability to generate faith that it is best suited and committed to work towards this vision define a political brand's relationship with its constituents.

One party may envision a country that constantly embraces modernity with progressive values while another party may have a vision of the nation sticking to traditional values and slowly adopting modernity. One party may have a vision of a socially equal country while another may have a vision based on individuals earning more based on their abilities.

Directly linked to the vision are the values based on which the vision is to be translated to reality. While two parties may have a common vision of their nation being economically developed, one party may believe this objective should be achieved through self-sufficiency, while another may look at achieving this in a shorter time frame through assistance from partner nation states.

But while vision and values are important, almost equally important is the brand's ability to reach out to their core audience. Some parties use segmenting tactics to build a small but loyal base like the Communist Party has in India, while others with larger aspirations try to maintain a strong relationship with a bigger audience by providing multiple facets to their vision and appealing to their audience at different levels. Most big parties try to cover a wide audience by choosing as their candidates representatives of various ethnic groups, religions, etc. Some parties even choose gay candidates to show their broad-mindedness and support of key issues.

The difference between political parties is often the party's perspective towards key issues and the means of addressing these issues. The key issues that a political party identifies at any point of time are often a reflection of its perspective and character. While some of the more traditional issues are unemployment, abortion, taxation, which almost always strike an emotional chord with voters, there are also more complex issues that may not be immediately evident as key issues.

These issues could pertain to the environment, development of alternative sources of energy, etc. and the brand constituents probably would need to be educated on the importance of these issues. A party's ability to make its electorate see the relevance of key issues shows its understanding and ability to make its audience relate to the party. The party's willingness to take up these issues instead of focusing only on more basic emotional issues shows the brand's stature and maturity.

Strong political brands show their strength of character in their decisions. The wisdom not to rush into a decision and the maturity to understand the implications of any decision taken reflect the party's priorities. The true test of character comes when the party has to take unpopular decisions in the interest of the country. This shows the party's selflessness, a good attribute for a brand to have given that political parties need to have a long term focus. Political parties that convincingly explain the reason behind their actions tend to survive tough decisions.

In 1984 in UK the National Union of Miners went on strike to oppose the closure of their pits. The then Prime Minister Margaret Thatcher refused to give in to union demands – and won – but her decision was a tough and unpopular one. Mikhail Gorbachev's attempts at making the Soviet Union a more democratic country made him unpopular with conservatives who were still in positions of power, but he persisted with this line of thought. Tough decisions are necessary at times, and ducking them or being politically correct is not the route to becoming a strong brand.

The perceptions of a political party are often guided by the quality of people they have. John F. Kennedy, Franklin Roosevelt and Churchill were but a few politicians who added lustre to their party by their presence. Most parties do not have rigid selection criteria or enrolment drives, and therefore it is left to the strength of the brand's vision and the quality of party leadership to attract the right kind of workers in the required numbers. The selection policies show the party's recognition of merit, its belief in diversity and the nature of governance that it actually plans to offer.

Personalities play an important role in the branding of political parties. Often celebrities start political parties, such as the Telugu Desam party started by Telugu film actor N. T. Rama Rao in Andhra Pradesh. Similarly, famous personalities like film star Arnold Schwarznegger have added to the existing equity of their political parties, and this has worked to their advantage too. Celebrities cash in on their fame to draw audiences and sometimes votes. Ronald Reagan, the one- time-famous movie star, went on to become the President of the United States of America while Arnold Schwarznegger has become the Governor of California. Clint Eastwood, NBA star Bill Bradley, former Pakistani cricket great Imran Khan, football legend Pele all used their celebrity status to earn votes.

The truly successful political personalities are those who have built a rapport with their audience. Celebrity politicians know what expectations their constituents have from them and know how to tie this up to key issues. From here the ability to stir emotions and aspirations to the politicians' benefit is not too difficult. It can be tough to meet these expectations, which are often based on emotion and hero worship.

The importance of branding lies in the fact that it helps create a DNA structure or an internal logic for the party, so that everything that proceeds from it is consistent across time, place and party members. The vision builds a commonality of purpose and aligns all aspects of the party towards it. Evolved parties spend a lot of time in educating their workers about what the party stands for as they know the importance of ensuring clarity right from the ground level, and ensure consistency in thought and action.

A clear idea of the party vision and values helps party workers know what their party stance would be on any issue by relating it to the party vision and values. For example, party workers in a party that believes in peaceful mediation and uplifting of the downtrodden would know by and large what the party's stand would be on the topic of riots caused by frustrated unemployed people. Should the party sympathise, criticise or condone is a tough question, and waiting for the party's stance could mean a loss of opportunity for words or action. Understanding the party's internal logic and therefore its stand on any issue is critical for party members, and branding provides this internal clarity.

Branding benefits political parties the way it benefits any organisation by providing focus, clarity, consistency and a powerful relationship with constituents.

Branding can play an important role in the lives of politicians and political parties. Truly, it's no longer the last resort of politicians.

16

Developing a Well-Rounded Brand Personality

EVERYTHING that a brand does reveals a facet of its personality. Corporate brands display multiple facets – self-importance, generosity, a sense of humour, arrogance, greed, etc. to multiple audiences on a daily basis. Despite many a well-developed communication plan guaranteed to maximise favourable exposure, many brands are probably suffering because they are showing their wrong side to all their audiences. A glance at the daily newspapers or a look at the television shows that brands concentrate primarily on two audiences with two messages.

Brands tell customers in a variety of ways that they are a good choice – mainly through advertising. Corporate brands target investors and the financial community telling them about their performance and plans. It makes them about as interesting as a piece of chalk, as personable as a piece of straw and as multi-faceted as a razor blade.

Corporate brands are always on the lookout to sell to audiences and this makes them predictable and charmless. It gives them a uni-dimensional personality when what constituents want is a multi-faceted personality.

Brands that display multi-faceted personalities have 5 advantages:

1. They get a lot more attention and generate more conversation than other brands

Brands that show courage, humour, adventure and generosity

tend to get more free coverage and attention than others. Richard Branson's irreverent attitude and Virgin's battle with British Airways gave the Virgin brand interesting facets to its personality that made the brand more appealing to its constituents. The reportage of interesting facts and the ensuing conversation helps build involvement levels of the brands constituents.

2. They are forgiven sooner

Brands that have well-rounded personalities are seen as not being overtly money-minded. If one such brand faces a problem such as an accidental failure in quality, this brand will probably be forgiven more spontaneously, quickly and easily by its constituents who regard it as being more than just a money-focused, business-focused brand. Tylenol once had a product scare but J&J's role in helping mothers and families for years and its caring perspective probably helped remove any negative associations with the brand.

3. They get less flak for aggressive moves

People are less likely to react negatively to aggressive moves by a brand that has a multi-faceted personality. Moves from brands like Virgin may not be seen as predatory, while moves from brands that seem to lack vision and personality immediately appear predatory.

4. Gives an additional reason for associating with the brand

Many people associate with well-rounded corporate personalities. There are some who invest in a brand with only rudimentary knowledge of investing and a simple faith in the brand as was in the case of Ben & Jerry's public offering. 'It's a great company, got guts, you know,' was the sentiment. Others prefer the brand as consumers – 'I like Ben & Jerry's; it's got something about it that's different. It's just nice to support a fun loving cause driven company.'

5. Adds differentiation

One of the important benefits of a well-rounded brand personality is that it attracts attention and spurs debate leading to differentiation that is critical to the brand.

There are different ways in which brands can add to their corporate personality such as:

1. Support a cause

People love Ben and Jerry's for their generosity. Patagonia and The Body Shop are more than businesses – the cause they are related to has added a valuable facet to their brand personality by making these brands appear generous, caring and socially aware.

2. Take up an issue

Sam Walton took up the issue of supporting goods 'Made in America' and this added another dimension to the Wal-Mart brand as a strongly patriotic brand. This added a differentiation to the Wal-Mart brand and brought it further into the limelight.

3. Do something unexpected

Richard Branson flying around the world in a hot air balloon may not have been done as a brand-building stunt, but at the same time it added an element of adventure to the corporate personality of Virgin. Sam Walton dancing on the steps of Wall Street in a grass skirt after losing a bet showed a fun side to the brand.

4. Stand up to adversity or bullies

Chrysler stood up to adversity in a manner that surprised many across the world. Getting the government to provide a loan in the form of a bail-out package and all the events that led up to the loan showed the corporate brand's confidence and guts. The manner in which South West Airlines and Virgin Airways took on their larger competitors gave them a huge fan following as brands that resisted bullies and fought for their rights.

5. A dash of humour

South West Airlines and Ben & Jerry's are two outstanding examples of how brands can add a welcome dimension to their personality in terms of humour and fun.

Every brand has a variety of facets to its personality – some are appealing, some not so appealing, some are stark, some are rarely displayed, some surface under pressure. Only some facets can be managed as some facets are spontaneous. It is important for brands to look at their corporate personalities and see whether the personality is uni-dimensional and dry and what needs to be done that can improve their personality and brand equity. It is important to ensure that any measure to add facets to the corporate brand personality must be a natural facet of the brand and capable of being sustained.

17

What's Wrong with Brands These Days?

In recent times there has been a virtual explosion of information on the topic of branding. There are new ideas, insights and models being developed every minute as marketers try to identify an enduring method of building and sustaining the most precious asset of any organisation – its brand equity.

But while interesting new theories are being developed there are a lot of ugly traits being displayed. Leading brands have exhibited shameful practices, but these are symptomatic of a larger disorder. Here are some of the things brands are doing wrongly these days.

Lack of intent

Brands like Walt Disney and Harley Davidson have shown how powerful consumer focus can help even brands with scarce resources grow tremendously. Unfortunately, consumer focus does not seem to be popular amongst many brands today and most of the scams of big brands in the recent past can be traced back to greed. Enron and WorldComm are clear examples of brands who placed their own interests before that of their constituents.

When a brand shifts its focus from its consumers towards itself, the resultant impact on its equity can be disastrous. The shift in focus may appear to be gradual, even imperceptible. However, the gap in attitude internally develops very rapidly. This is probably because employees start realising that the brand itself does not have a moral standpoint or integrity which in turn gives these employees the confidence to indulge in their petty misdeeds.

Brand equity is a function of trust that constituents have in the brand and as brands look towards themselves more than looking towards their constituents, this trust starts eroding.

Misusing their power

Bullying/domineering/corrupt practices by brands are no longer uncommon and one increasingly sees brands using their size to crowd out smaller players from the market. The Microsoft– Netscape tussle was seen by many as an attempt by a strong brand to bully a smaller competitor. Crowding a competitor out of the market is not always a smart move and can be counterproductive.

In fact, competition often helps a brand understand how strong it truly is. Consumers choosing a brand for want of reliable options in terms of availability is not a true indicator of consumers' preference of the brand, and the sooner brand custodians stop fooling themselves about this, the better for themselves.

The wrong people handling the brand

One increasingly sees branding being handled in a cavalier fashion with new brand custodians changing the entire basis of the brand relationship with its consumers through ill-advised moves. With brand managers increasingly being responsible for driving sales, some companies have resorted to making their sales managers take over the branding portfolio. While this is not always a bad thing, it is however always important that a brand manager should be attitudinally inclined towards brand building and should have a KRA that is in line with the brand function.

P&G is one of the few extremely brand-focused companies and their recruitment processes reflect their appreciation of the importance of the role played by their brand managers.

CEO not involved enough

CEOs need to recognise that it is brand equity that ensures high sales and increased profitability in an organisation. In fact, a strong brand provides several advantages to an organisation beyond the sales and marketing benefits. Good brands attract high-quality talent, low-cost funding and keep the morale high. With brand equity playing such a valuable role for the organisation, it is important that CEOs take an active interest in ensuring that brand values are never compromised and that brand equity is maintained and grown.

Unfortunately, many CEOs do not give branding its due importance and only bother when it starts failing them. P&G, Pepsi and Coca-Cola are huge brands that have benefited from having highly brand-focused CEOs and are good examples for other brands to follow.

The lack of holistic focus

Increasingly, brands are seen as having an organisational interface rather than only a marketing connotation. It is, therefore, not enough for the brand manager to do his job well – there is a need for the non-marketing functions to back up the brand at different levels. Financial scams, non-conformance to ethical production norms, etc. can harm the brand by showing that the brand does not live up to what it professes.

Arthur Andersen, Enron and WorldComm are reputed brands that are answering embarrassing questions for reasons that are not quite related to marketing.

Brands that do not actively disseminate information on their brand values across the organisation and stress on the need to live up to the professed values will find that the non-marketing functions can erode brand equity faster than the marketing department can build it.

Lack of strong-mindedness and adequate belief

Brands are under constant pressure to deliver greater and greater returns to their investors. Often brand custodians feel that they need to do something different to break the shackles of slow growth or negative growth. It is important for brand custodians to have the belief that their offering has the necessary resilience to last out a tough period. Harley Davidson is a brand that survived a near death experience because of its self-belief, but many other brands have thrown in the towel with a whimper.

In India the market leader in colas, Thums Up, quickly sold out to Coke when cola majors Pepsi and Coke moved into India. This probably was a short-sighted move displaying a total lack of self-belief in Thums Up's ability to stand up to competition. Close to ten years after the sale, Thums Up still occupies a prime position in the Indian market and has not got wiped out as expected by many.

Lack of concern

As more and more brands are seen damaging the environment, faking test results and exploiting their employees/associates, there is a distinct possibility that brands will be seen as faceless money-making machines with no finer side to them.

It is difficult for consumers to believe that the same brand that would callously poison the environment in the course of production would have genuine concern for their consumers. If a brand is seen as lacking concern towards one set of human beings, it is difficult for the same brand to have concern for another set of human beings. The consequent cynicism directed towards brands in general and 'guilty' brands in particular can undermine the entire belief structure that branding is based on.

The presence of a few brands with outstanding humane practices like Levis unfortunately does not make up for the growing number of unconcerned brands.

Lack of focus

Many brand custodians have lost the primary focus of branding. More and more brands are providing a rational reason for consumers to purchase them rather than an emotional reason. The reliance on marketing exercises that build equity and lure consumers have been replaced with exercises that drive sales through discounts, price-offs and contests. Branding is all about providing an emotional difference that draws the consumer rather than providing a rational reason to buy the brand. It is often easier to provide a discount than build a compelling desire to buy the brand at the same or even higher rate. The innumerable 'deals' one witnesses of even well-established brands in a routine supermarket visit is testimony to this.

Brand custodians have to get back to the basics. Genuine intent backed by sound values and foolproof systems is the only way to create enduring brand equity. There are no short-cuts to reach this destination. Supping on the goose that lays the golden eggs is as unwise as it gets.